# DESIGN CONCEPTS AND APPLICATIONS

**Reproduced on the Cover**

Frank Cheatham, *South Coast.* 1969.

Magnesite, Acrylic, Wood, 12″ × 22″ × 6″

**Cover Photograph**

Robert Suddarth

**Cover Design**

Frank Cheatham

DESIGN CONCEPTS AND APPLICATIONS

Professor, Department of Art, Texas Tech University

FRANK R. CHEATHAM

Assistant Professor, Division of Architecture, Texas Tech University

JANE HART CHEATHAM

Visiting Lecturer, Department of Art, Texas Tech University

SHERYL A. HALER

PRENTICE-HALL, INC., ENGLEWOOD CLIFFS, N.J.

Library of Congress Cataloging in Publication Data

Cheatham, Frank.
      Design concepts and applications.

      Includes index.
         1. Design.   I. Cheatham, Jane.   II. Haler, Sheryl.
III. Title.
NK1510.C457 1983        701'.8        82-12332
ISBN   0-13-201897-7


**Productions Editor:** Dee Amir Josephson
**Manufacturing Buyer:** Harry Baisley
**Designers:** Frank Cheatham, Jane Cheatham, Sheryl Haler
**Illustrators:** Jane Cheatham, Frank Cheatham

Printed in the United States of America


10  9  8  7  6  5  4  3  2  1
ISBN 0-13-201897-7

Prentice-Hall International, Inc., *London*
Prentice-Hall of Australia Pty. Limited, *Sydney*
Prentice-Hall do Brazil, Ltda., *Rio de Janeiro*
Prentice-Hall Canada, *Toronto*
Prentice-Hall of India Private Limited, *New Delhi*
Prentice-Hall of Japan, Inc., *Tokyo*
Prentice-Hall of Southeast Asia Pte. Ltd., *Singapore*
Whitehall Books Limited, *Wellington, New Zealand*

# CONTENTS

# INTRODUCTION

We have intended *Design Concepts and Application* to meet the educational needs of those who are beginning to study and apply design in the visual arts—either two or three dimensionally. It incorporates those elements, tangible and intangible, that form the foundation of design as applied in the visual arts.

In abbreviated terms, *design* means to plan or to scheme. This basic definition is quite flexible. It can include the very broad, as in "the grand design," or the more specific, like architectural design. We can use "to plan" or "to scheme" as a simplified, general definition of design, but we could also formulate more complicated and specific definitions. One, for example, could be this: "A design is a plan to make something: something we can see or hold or walk into; something that is two-dimensional or three dimensional, and sometimes in the time dimension. It is always something seen and sometimes something touched, and now and then by association, something heard. It is often a single item and just as often a mass-produced product."* However, whether design is looked at very simply or in a more complex way, it always involves planning. This system or procedure is frequently called the *design process*.

The design process basically involves the consideration of abstract and concrete, intangible and tangible, elements. In the visual arts, elements such as space, composition, and contrast are the tangible and visible tools used to design the appearance of a work. The intangible elements include the area of communication, idea, and content. In the design process, these intangible elements provide the basis for selecting and manipulating the tangible components. Ultimately, both intangible and tangible elements interact to create the whole visual expression. So when designing a visual expression, the artist must be consciously aware of and familiar with all the basic components of design. In summary we can say that design in art involves a planning process whereby both intangible and tangible components are selected, manipulated, and synthesized to create a whole visual expression—a work of art.

---

*The Partners of Pentagram, *Living by Design* (London: Lund Humphries, 1978), p. 7.

# SECTION ONE

# 1

## GESTALT

The fields of psychology and visual art share several areas of investigative interest. One of these is *visual perception*.

For a number of years, psychologists have been interested in determining how the human eye and brain function together in the process of perception. As artists, we also are interested in this topic because our visual expressions are ultimately intended to be perceived by others.

One set of psychological studies and resulting theories of perception is called Gestalt psychology. Some of these principles do not affect us directly as artists. However, many of the Gestalt investigations and theories seem to have logical and practical application in the visual arts. These deal with the notion that all of us have a basic desire for unity and harmony. Simply stated, the basic principle is this: Images are first perceived as unified wholes before they are perceived as parts. This means we "see" the whole before we "see" the parts that make up the whole.

Gestalt psychologists have concluded that the perceptual capabilities of a viewer are such that the eye/brain does not initially differentiate each of the individual component parts of an image. Instead, it will organize the components into a more comprehensible, unified whole. Additionally, Gestalt theory maintains that within a gestalt (a single field of vision or a single frame of reference), the eye has the capacity to absorb only a limited number of unrelated whole units. This capacity is dependent on the units' visual differences, similarities, and relative positions. The following diagrams and explanations are intended to illustrate Gestalt theory and to show how it can be used in a visual art context to create unity and harmony.

Figure 1 is an example of a single gestalt consisting of two whole units. Each of these units is made up of several individual, but still unified, parts. Although each of the individual parts is distinctly separate and visually unique, the eye/brain simplifies them into two whole units. Each unit is perceptually unified due to the relative positioning of its parts.

1

If we are confronted with too many unrelated units in a single gestalt, the eye/brain attempts to simplify the gestalt by organizing the various units into a perceptually manageable whole. When this is not possible, the image will continue to appear unorganized or chaotic. For example, Figure 2 contains several whole units that are totally unrelated in size and position. The visual effect is that of a haphazard, disorganized arrangement of shapes. In Figure 3, these same units have been visually organized into three unified groups, so this figure appears more organized and less chaotic than Figure 2. Figure 4 presents the same units in still another whole configuration that becomes the recognizable image of a horse. This image seems less chaotic than those in Figure 2 or Figure 3. In Figure 4, the whole unit "horse" is apparent to us before we become aware of the complexity of the horse's various parts and their relationships.

Clearly, then, Gestalt theory proposes that the eye/brain is continually involved in an organizing, simplifying, and unifying process that produces a comprehensible and harmonious whole.

Artists have long realized the importance of presenting a sense of unity and harmony in their works. From intuitive contemplation and conscious evaluation of their own expressions and viewer responses, artists have concluded that neither they nor their viewers will respond positively to disorganized imagery. When confronted with an image or form that has a poor gestalt

2

3

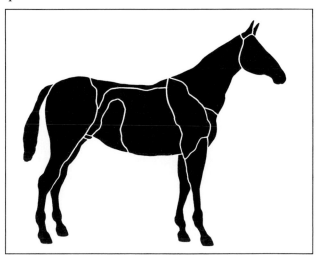

4

(an image lacking visual unity or harmony), the viewer finds the visual effect unrelated, busy, or disturbing. This creates the impression that "something is wrong." Consequently, the image will be ignored or rejected by the viewer.

The task for us as artists, then, is visually to organize the existing elements of an image so they create a comprehensible whole. To accomplish this, the following elementary methods for simplifying, organizing, and unifying images or forms have been developed: deletion, proximity, overall pattern, closure, alignment, and similarity.

## DELETION

Deletion consists of consciously removing nonessential material from the visual statement so only those components that are absolutely necessary remain. This results in visual simplification. Figure 5, *Head of an*

*Idol,** from the Cycladic Islands, is an outstanding illustration of deletion that results in a simplified, elegant form.

While creating a visual expression, it may be helpful to ask this question: "Do I have any extraneous components in the image that may interfere with my intended expression?" If the answer is "yes," why not take them out to improve the gestalt of the visual statement? When asking this question, bear in mind that an interesting, intriguing, or engaging visual statement need not be visually complex. Many intriguing works are visually very simple, as exemplified by the Rembrandt painting in Figure 6.

5

*Head of An Idol,* from Island of Amorgos, Cyclades, Collection Louvre, Paris

6

Rembrandt, *Self-Portrait,* National Gallery of Art, Washington, Widener Collection

*The examples used throughout the text are not meant to be suggestive of the individual artist's conscious *intent* in conceiving and executing his or her work. Rather, they are intended to illustrate in visual form what is being discussed verbally in order to assist in greater clarity of comprehension.

Another common method of deletion is *cropping*. This is a process of covering up, or blocking from view, a portion of the whole image to enable us to see a new visual frame of reference. Cropping an image is a quick method of visualizing any portion of it in a new arrangement. There are several advantages to deleting by cropping. It is usually easier than outright deletion; it is also more flexible, less time-consuming, and does not seem to be so irrevocably final. Due to the temporary nature of cropping, it is easy to delete various areas without fear of making an irrevocable error in judgment or of losing the original image.

Two methods of cropping are shown in Figures 7 and 8. In Figure 7, two 90 degree angles have been cut out of stiff opaque paper to form two separate L shapes. These shapes can be moved independently or simultaneously over any two-dimensional image to create a new proportion and a new image. Also, they can be placed over an image to block temporarily from view those components that may not be contributing significantly to the overall expression. Figure 8 shows a similar method of visualizing the deletion of a component or components. This method may be used on larger two-dimensional and three-dimensional works, such as paintings, tapestries, and sculptures. Using this technique, we simply block from view with our finger or hand any portion of a work that may be in question. If the image appears more unified without the blocked area, then deletion of that component should be considered to create a more unified gestalt.

7

8

## PROXIMITY

When individual visual units are next to or near one another, they can be described as being in *proximity* and are usually seen as grouped. The various methods of visual grouping by proximity are direct and easily performed. The artist can use them independently or in as many numbers and combinations as necessary to create a well-organized gestalt.

### Close-Edge Relation

In Figure 9, visual units have been moved closer and closer together. At some point, the space separating the edges of the units becomes so small that instead of separating, the units visually lock. When this happens, the individual units may be seen as a larger whole consisting of smaller individual ones. This is close-edge relation by proximity.

Visual grouping by close-edge relation can occur just as easily for large numbers of dissimilar units as for small numbers of similar units. For example, in Figure 10, even though most of the individual units are unrelated in size and shape, they have been simplified and organized into three groups of larger whole units. In this case, each of the larger whole units is primarily unified by the close-edge relation created by the proximity of the various parts. (Secondarily, it is unified by the visual similarity of color and value—another method to be discussed later.)

Even if individual units are not similar or identical in color and value—as they are in Figure 11—visually they will still group. In this example, the unity of the three whole units may seem diminished, but it is certainly not destroyed. Through close-edge relation, the individual units remain organized into three visually manageable wholes.

9

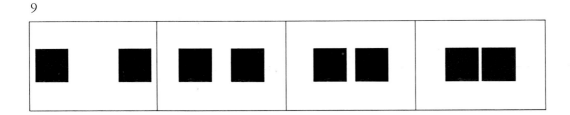

10

11

To achieve visual grouping, an unknown pre-Columbian artist from ancient Mexico has used close-edge relation in designing a flat clay stamp (Figure 12). Despite the fact that the individual units do not touch and vary dramatically in shape, size, and position, they are all organized by close-edge relation into two easily discernible whole groups.

The poster designed by Arnold Sacks (Figure 13) to announce an inflatable sculpture exhibition uses close-edge relation to help communicate the concept of "inflatable." The heavy lines positioned close together toward the bottom and sides of the poster visually separate as they gradually move farther apart in the center. As a result of the fluid nature of the lines and the configurations caused by the separation, the lines actually appear to have been inflated in the center while being held firmly together at the sides.

12

Flat clay stamp, Courtesy Dover Publications, Inc., *Design Motifs of Ancient Mexico* by Jorge Enciso

13. Poster designed by Arnold Saks for The Jewish Museum, New York

In order to separate and clarify printed verbal concepts, typographic design often incorporates visual grouping by close-edge relation. The book cover (Figure 14) is a classic example. In this case, the close-edge relation occurs between individual letters, words, and lines of type to cause the typographic whole to be separated into two visual groups—the author's name as one group, and the book title in three languages as another.

## Combining

Individual units cannot be more closely associated than when they are physically *combined*. There are several useful ways of combining individual units. The most obvious is to place smaller units inside larger ones so that the visual boundaries of a larger unit serve as a container for the smaller ones. For example, because of combining, the multiple units in Figure 15 appear more organized and simplified than those in Figure 16.

Another example of this method of combining can be seen in the mysterious photograph by Jerry Uelsmann, *All American Tree* (Figure 17). Despite the number and variety of the individual units—there are over forty, excluding the leaves—the photograph has a strong unified gestalt. This is achieved by combining all the smaller units inside four larger ones. The light value of the sky creates three major units. The fourth unit is created by the dark shape of the tree and foreground. Each of these four parts contains smaller units of controlled value that give the photograph its overall visual strength.

14

**J. Müller-Brockmann**

**Gestaltungsprobleme des Grafikers
The Graphic Artist and his Design Problems
Les problèmes d'un artiste graphique**

Book cover designed by J. Müller-Brockmann

15

16

Jerry N. Uelsmann, *All American Tree,* 1965

A third example of combining is Paul Rand's book cover (Figure 18), which consists of eleven individual units. The photograph of the rocket and the seven lines of type are organized into a single unit by placing the individual components within the boundaries of a large captial R.

**Touching**

A variation of combining by proximity is touching. When individual units are placed close enough to actually touch one another, the units will visually form a larger, unified whole. For example, Figure 19 contains several individual units that are dissimilar in shape and value. When these units are brought close enough to touch one another, as in Figure 20, they become visu-

18

Cover design by Paul Rand
From *The Anatomy of Revolution,* by Crane Brinton.
Published 1965 by Alfred A. Knopf, Inc.

19

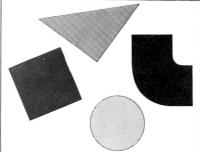

20

21

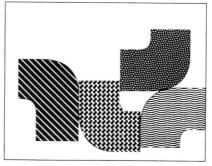

22

ally unified as a single group. In addition, if units similar in shape and value, but dissimilar in color or texture (Figure 21), are brought close enough to touch one another, they will also visually "unite."

In Figures 20 and 21, each individual component maintains its unique identity. In Figure 22, dissimilarities in shape, color, value, or texture have become so pronounced that the visual unity of the whole is weakened. However, touching has prevented the whole from being completely disunified. Conversely, in Figure 23, units that are different in shape but identical in color, value, or texture have almost lost their identity. This is a result of touching. When this happens, the larger group is almost certain to have a stronger visual unity than its individual parts.

Architecture, because of its assembled and constructive nature, frequently utilizes the principle of touching to achieve visual unity. See, for example, Figure 24 the façade of the Israeli Pavilion in Montreal. The stepping-stone, rectangular volumes unify this handsome façade as a result of physical and visual touching.

By effectively grouping individual components by touching, the artist Norman Laliberte has created an engaging visual statement with flat shapes of a single color (Figure 25). In this illustration, the touching shapes create an overall image of a man wearing a hat next to a tulip. Because of touching, the individual units are not only unified, but visually more interesting.

25

Norman Laliberte, Courtesy Art Education, Inc., N.Y.

23

24. Israeli Pavilion at Expo 67, Montreal. Architect, Arieh Sharon

Another example of the unity that can be attained by having individual units touch is seen in the bas-relief sculpture by Frank Cheatham in Figure 26. Even though this sculpture physically contains more than two hundred individual components, visually it can be simplified into four parts. Three of the four are unified as whole groups as a result of touching.

26

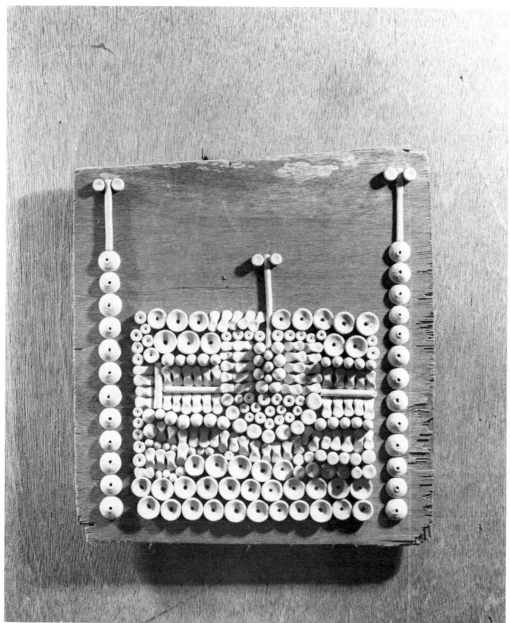

Frank Cheatham, *Map For Another World,* 1974

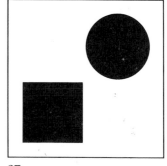

27

## Overlapping

Overlapping is another variation of combining. Individual units become visually attached to one another because they are physically overlapped (Figure 27). The strength of this visual attachment can be controlled by certain variables. For instance, the closer in value, color, or texture the units are, the more visually welded they will appear (Figures 28 and 29). If all the units are exactly the same in value, color, or texture, the dividing outlines of the individual configurations will disappear and a single shape will be created' (Figure 30).

In addition to value, color, or texture, transparent and three-dimensional objects can be used to create visual unity by overlapping. In Figure 31, the visual result of overlapping transparent units can be seen. Even if they are not physically attached, three-dimensional objects can be arranged in a variety of ways to appear visually overlapped and unified. For example, they can be placed in proximity so they appear to overlap when viewed from certain positions, as in Figure 32. The use of overlapping is successful when we can view the overall configuration of the three-dimensional objects as having a common, unified outline.

Photographer: Maggy Cuesta

28
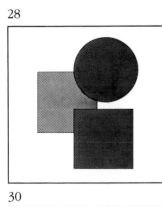

29
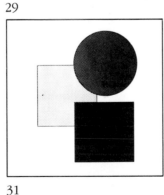

30

31
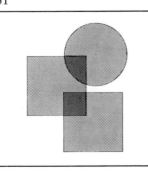

## OVERALL PATTERN AND/OR TEXTURE

Both patterns and textures are composed of multiple, repetitive units. The major difference between the two is size or scale; in all other physical respects, they are basically the same. A pattern is a visually magnified texture, and a texture is a visually reduced pattern. For this reason, except in cases that require a specific distinction, we can discuss pattern and texture simultaneously.

The perception of a visual gestalt as a pattern or texture is always based on size and scale, but depending on the situation, other factors may also have an effect. For example, the number of overall units in a gestalt can control the appearance of a pattern or texture. This visual phenomenon can occur when the number of individual units is so great that they cannot easily be perceived as individuals. Leaves viewed from a window could be big enough to make a pattern, but if there is a large quantity of them, we may see them as a texture instead (Figure 33).

In addition to number, pattern and texture can be determined by the physical qualities of the units. If they appear raised from the surface enough that they appeal to the sense of touch, the units could suggest a tactile

33

Photographer: Marty Robins

34

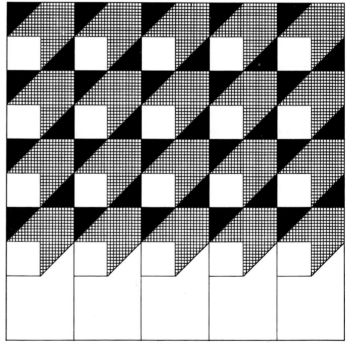

physical quality. Depending on size and scale, this quality might make a pattern seem textural, it might make a texture appear to be a pattern, or it could create a texture within a pattern so that both exist simultaneously (Figure 34).

These are just two factors—number and physical quality—of many that can have an effect on the visual perception of pattern or texture.

Patterns and textures can be created in either two or three dimensions from anything that can be repeated (Figures 35 and 36). They can be created by the repeti-

35

Photographer: Maggy Cuesta

36. Marty Robins, *Carnival Man,* 1981

tion of similar or dissimilar individual units placed in proximity. This is done by arranging *all* the parts of a gestalt close enough visually so that they are perceived as a single patterned or textured area instead of as distinctly individual units. Figure 37 shows a group of similar and dissimilar visual units organized so the single overall gestalt is perceived as a pattern rather than as individual components. Another example of this is the decorated Acoma Pueblo jar shown in Figure 38.

37

38. Acoma Pueblo Jar by Lucy Lewis, Photograph by Bobby Hanson, New York

When it is necessary to present a number of visually different units, the pattern and texture device can be used to organize and unify a gestalt. The contemporary illustrator Fred Otnes often uses this method to organize his complex visual statements (Figure 39). Even though a wide variety of individual units are included in this gestalt, they appear to be strongly unified. An overall pattern/texture is created by the light and dark values of the images, as well as the consistent repetition of predominantly square or rectangular shapes.

39. Cover of a booklet on the planning of newspaper advertising issued by Newspaper Advertising Bureau. Artist: Fred Otnes

Overall pattern and texture is often used by primitive artists as a method of visual unification. In Figure 40, dark linear elements have been used repetitively to create an overall pattern and texture that successfully unify the form. The Paul Klee drawing, *Architecture in Ruins* (Figure 41), is also composed of a number of linear, geometric shapes in proximity. They create an overall pattern/texture that is perceived before the viewer is aware of the various individual units that make it up.

40

41

Paul Klee, *Architecture in Ruins,* 1938, ©1981, Copyright by COSMOPRESS, Geneva & *ADAGP,* Paris

Helmet Mask, Songe Tribe Tetela; Africa, Congo.
Dallas Museum of Fine Arts, The Clark and Frances Stillman Collection of Congo Sculpture, A Gift of Eugene and Margaret McDermott

## CLOSURE

Another common method of visual grouping is based on the human ability to complete partial images. This perceptual phenomenon is called *closure:* We perceive an incomplete image as complete by mentally filling in missing pieces. For example, Figure 42 can be perceived as a completed circle rather than just three curved lines; Figure 43 is easily identifiable as the image of a human face although many of its parts are missing.

Of course, our ability to see the parts of an image as a complete whole depends on the nature of the image and the relationship of its parts. For instance, if the nature of an image is such that it is unrecognizable even when complete, it will surely remain unrecogniz-

able when many of its parts are missing. If too many parts of an image are missing (Figure 45), there may be an insufficient number of visible clues to assemble the image into a recognizable whole. If the parts of an image are too far apart (Figure 44), the distance that must be closed perceptually may be too great. In all these cases, the parts continue to be perceived as individual units complete in themselves.

42

43

44

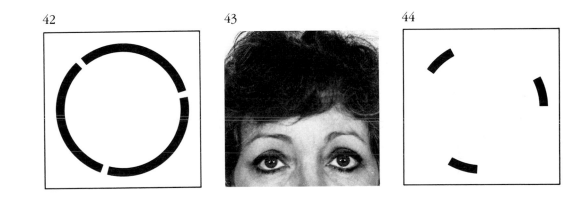

45

## ALIGNMENTS AND GRID SYSTEMS

In design, the term *alignment* can be defined simply as "lined up." Thus, when two or more units can be perceived as being lined up, they are aligned.

There are two ways we can achieve alignment—physically and optically. A *physical* alignment occurs when two or more units are placed on a physically perceivable common line (Figure 46). An optical alignment differs from a physical alignment in only one respect; the common line aligning the units is not physically included in the visual image. This imaginary line visually, rather than physically, aligns the various units (Figure 47). A good example of optical alignment can be seen in the text on this page. The words being read align on a series of common lines that do not physically exist. This perceptual phenomenon is made operable by the gestalt closure principle, as well as the principle of proximity.

We can use physical and optical alignments to organize or to relate visually individual units, to position components, and to clarify or structure visual material. When two or more alignments are used in a given gestalt, they combine to create another organizational tool—the *grid*. A grid system is:

1. A method of dividing available two- or three-dimensional space into proportional parts.

2. A skeletal structure that holds all the parts of a designed area, or image, together in the same way that the human skeleton supports the various parts of the body.

3. A series of predetermined alignments and coordinates used as a plan for assembling visual material.

4. A modular, structural system used to unify and organize a wide variety or large number of individual units.

Grid systems have been used to organize, unify, and structure visual art since ancient times. They have been used by artists from primitive and from civilized societies, and they are still in constant use today. Grids are used in studio and applied art for both representational and abstract images. They are used by artists, designers, and craftspeople both consciously and intuitively.

The grids used by artists, designers, and craftspeople are all determined by individual needs and tastes. The visual product is a direct result of the effectiveness of the individual's judgment. Since there are an infinite number of ways to divide any given space or area, there are an infinite number of available grid systems. For purposes of discussion, however, we can divide these systems into five major categories that can be applied individually or in a variety of combinations:

46

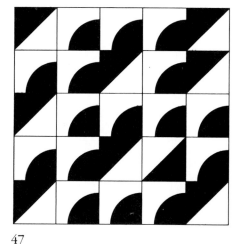

47

1. Visible grid. A grid system that is physically visible in the completed gestalt and was used in its execution (Figure 48).

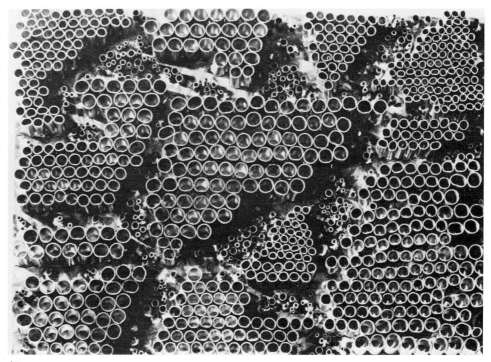

48. Zoltan Kemeny, *Study from Nature,* Kunstmuseum Hannover mit Sammlung Sprengel

2. Invisible grid. A grid system that is not physically visible in the completed gestalt, but was used in its execution (Figure 49).

49. Bell System Signage Manual designed by Saul Bass for AT&T

3 Rigid grid. A grid system composed of strait, linear divisions (Figure 50).

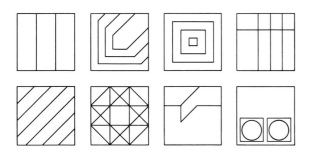

Yvonne Jacquette, *The Barn Window Sky,*
Courtesy of Brooke Alexander, Inc.

4. Organic grid. A grid system composed of curvilinear divisions (Figure 51).

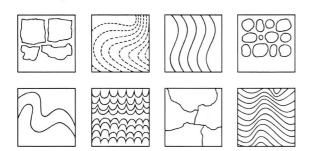

Primitive Mask. African, Zaire, Luba. Wood.
Metropolitan Museum of Art,
The Michael C. Rockefeller Memorial Collection,
Bequest of Nelson A. Rockefeller, 1979

5. Combined rigid and organic grid. A grid system composed of a combination of straight and curvilinear divisions (Figures 52 and 53).

52

Primitive Beaker, Americas, Coastal Huari, Tiahuanaco. Wood.
The Metropolitan Museum of Art, The Michael C. Rockefeller Memorial
Collection, Gift of Nelson A. Rockefeller, 1978

Gunther Haese, *Olymp.* 1967,
Collection Solomon R. Guggenheim
Museum, New York,
Photo, Robert Mates

53

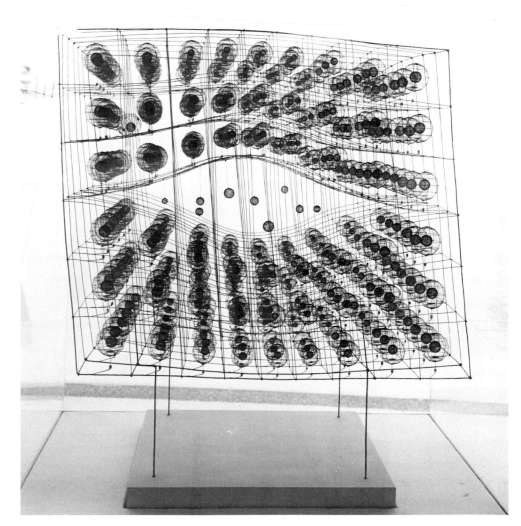

54

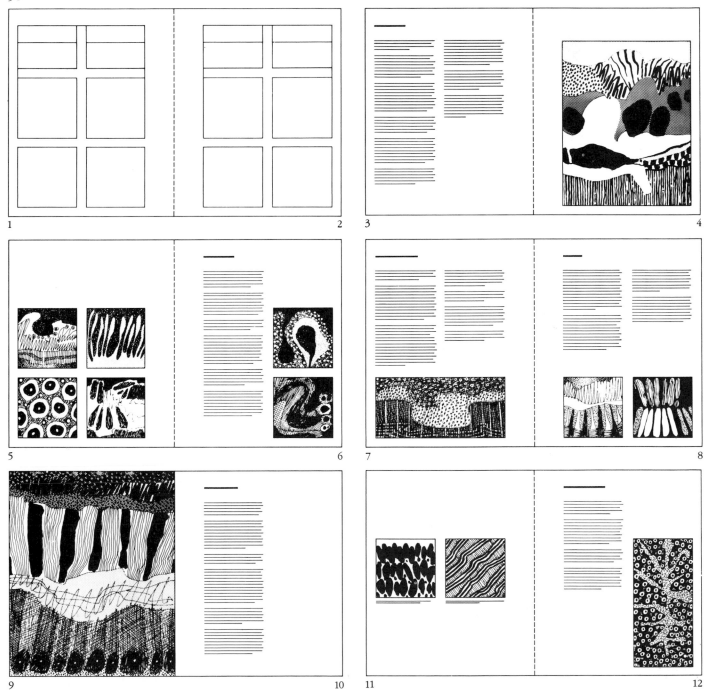

In applied design, the designer uses *modular* grid systems to give cohesiveness and continuity to visual material in serial presentations such as consecutive pages in a book or magazine, consecutive panels in an exhibit or signage program. Grid systems for serial design are as plentiful as the grids that divide individual spaces and areas. However, selection of an appropriate grid is somewhat less arbitrary, since the grid must be flexible enough to incorporate all the material (words, photographs, drawings, charts) to be included in the completed work. Figure 54 is an example of a modular grid system used in a book to relate the pages. Even though each double-page spread has different types of visual material, all the pages have a continuity based on the structure of the grid.

As with most things, there are exceptions. Even though a grid system is being used to organize material, it is sometimes physically or esthetically necessary to disregard the grid. Page nine of Figure 54 is an example; the large photograph bleeding off three edges of the page and touching the fold or gutter is used for a dramatic change of pace. If grid violations are kept to a minimum, they will not destroy the continuity of the whole and can often enhance the finished product. An expanded example of a modular grid structure used for consecutive page design can be seen by examining the pages of this text, which are based on the grid shown in Figure 55.

55

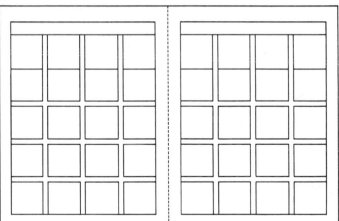

## SIMILARITY

Individual units have a tendency to group visually when they share common characteristics. This method of visual simplification is called grouping by similarity, and we can achieve it in a number of ways—size, shape or volume, direction, and color or value.

57. Henri Matisse, *Tree,* 1951, © S.P.A.D.E.M., Paris/V.A.G.A., New York, 1981

## Size

When individual units appear similar in size, they seem to belong together. And when the units look as if they belong together, it is easy to perceive them as being part of a larger visual grouping.

For example, Figure 56 contains ten individual squares. At first glance, the fact that there are squares, large and small, is more apparent than the fact that there are ten individual ones. This perception of "large and small" allows the complex image to be simplified mentally by size into two distinct groups. In fact, when consciously counting the squares, visual grouping probably would be used. The larger squares would be counted as a group and then the smaller ones.

Similarity of size was often used by Henri Matisse in complex works of art. A good example can be seen in his work, *Tree* (Figure 57). In this ink and gouache drawing, similarity of size has been used as the primary organizational device. The composition appears to be divided by the central tree trunk into two whole groups. The leaves as well as the branches on either side of the trunk are all similar in size. This size similarity causes all the individual units to group visually; in turn, this creates a strongly organized and unified gestalt.

A detail from the frieze on the Arch of Constantine (Figure 58) also uses similarity of size as a method of simplifying and organizing by visual grouping. Although there are a total of fifteen human figures in this detail, the viewer is primarily aware of two groups because of the positioning of the central figure. This seated figure can be seen as an individual or, because of its size and elevation, can be grouped visually with the figures on the right.

56

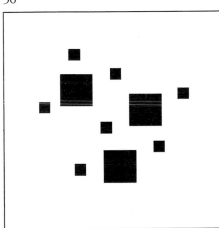

58

*People Listening to Constantine,* detail of arch of Constantine, AD 312-15 Rome, Courtesy Academy Editions, London

## Shape Or Volume

Units that have a similar shape or volume tend to be perceived as a group. Figure 59 consists of seven individual shapes. Three of the shapes are circular, and this common characteristic allows these shapes to be perceived as a group. The remaining four are triangular, and this similarity visually groups these shapes. The whole image tends to be perceived as a single gestalt divided into two groups consisting of circles and triangles.

The handsome sculptural form by Sheryl Haler, Figure 60, consists entirely of cylindrical forms that vary only in size. This configuration maintains its visual strength and unity through the use of similarity of volume.

59

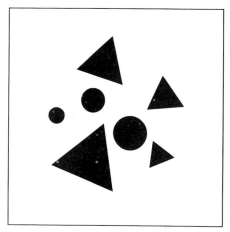

60. Sheryl Haler, *The Hunters,* 1981

The visual complexity of the interior of the mosque at Cordoba, Spain (Figure 61), would create a chaotic impression if divergent visual characteristics could not be simplified by grouping. In this interior, it is possible to group the gestalt into three parts based on similarity of shape and volume. The rectangular floor tiles are one group, the vertical columns form another group, and the various arches create the third grouping.

In *Les Promenades d'Euclide* (Figure 62), the Surrealist painter René Magritte has made an interesting use of similar shapes. The conical roof of the tower on the left is similar in shape to the thoroughfare between the buildings on the right. Also, the shape of the window and of the canvas form a perceptual grouping because of their similarity.

61

Mosque, Cordoba, Spain, 8th and 9th centuries.
Courtesy, MAS, Barcelona

62. Rene Margritte, *Les Promenades d'Euclide,* The Minneapolis Institute of Arts

## Direction

Various lines, shapes, and forms can appear similar if they can be perceived as traveling in the same direction. If we place single units so they seem to be moving in a similar direction, we will find that the units tend visually to group as a larger whole.

Figure 63 consists of individual rectangles. Because of their elongated shape, these rectangles appear to be moving in a horizontal or vertical direction. We can perceive those appearing to travel horizontally as one group, while those seeming to move vertically can be perceived as another.

Bridget Riley's painting (Figure 64) is a wonderful example of the motion that can be created by repetitive placement of lines sharing similarity of direction. In this case, the overall gestalt is one of a single rectangle divided by vertical wavy lines that appear to undulate. In addition, the gestalt is divided into horizontal concave and convex groups. These seem to be traveling in opposite horizontal directions—some are perceived as moving to the right and some to the left.

In the same way, Janet Fish's painting *8 Vinegar Bottles* (Figure 65) contains components that seem to move in a similar direction. Except for the diagonal direction of the few labels and the horizontal proportion of the picture plane, all the bottles create a vigorous vertical direction that unifies the gestalt of this work.

64

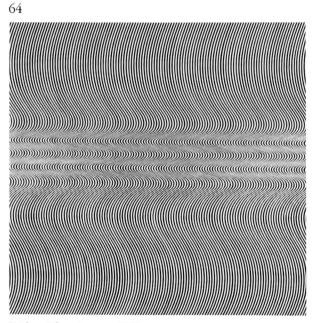

Bridget Riley, *Current,* 1964
Synthetic polymer paint on composition board, 58 3/8 x 58 7/8".
Collection, The Museum of Modern Art, New York.
Philip Johnson Fund

63

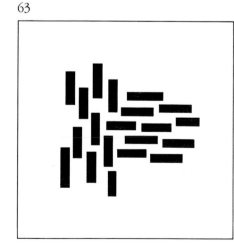

65

Janet Fish, *8 Vinegar Bottles,* 1972–73,
Dallas Museum of Fine Arts,
Gift of the 500, Inc.

### Color Or Value

The perception of individual units as part of a larger visual group occurs most often when units share a similar color or value. (The term *value* refers to the tonal quality of "lightness" or "darkness" of a color, or gray).

Figure 66 consists of a number of individual squares in two values of gray, light and dark. The squares sharing a common value are easily perceived as a visual group.

Unification through the use of similarity of color and value is beautifully exemplified in Eastman Johnson's charming painting *Five Boys on a Wall* (Figure 67). Even though there are eight separate elements—five boys, a wall, grass, and sky—the artist simplified and unified the work by repeating the dark values of the wall in various areas in the clothing and shadows on the figures. In this way the viewer readily sees three units—a wall with figures, grass, and sky.

66

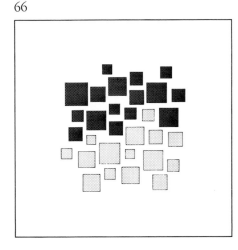

Eastman Johnson, *Five Boys on a Wall,* 1875–80, Dallas Museum of Fine Arts, Foundation for the Arts Collection, gift of Mr. and Mrs. George V. Charlton, Mrs. Alfred Bromberg, and Mr. Roland S. Bond

67

# SECTION ONE

2

COMPOSITION

When the various parts of an image in a completed visual expression have been consciously arranged within the boundaries of the image area, the result is a *composition*. And, since the whole of anything is structured by its parts and composition is an arrangement of the parts of a whole, it can be defined as a method of structuring. In the visual arts, then, a comprehensive definition of composition would be this: Composition is a method of structuring used to organize the component parts of a whole image.

There is no real difference in the application of this definition to two- and three-dimensional compositions. The boundaries of two-dimensional compositions are determined naturally by the edges of a two-dimensional surface, such as paper, illustration board, canvas. The area designated by the boundaries of a two-dimensional work is referred to by a number of interchangeable terms. Several of the most widely used are *frame of reference, picture plan, negative space,* and *ground.* The component parts of the total image within the two-dimensional composition are commonly called *figures* or *positive spaces* (Figure 1).

Frame of Reference,
Picture Plane or Ground

Negative Space

Positive Space, Figure

1

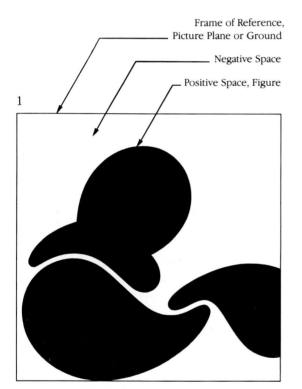

Negative Space

Positive Space, Figure
or Component

2

Giacomo Manzu, *Young Girl on a Chair,* 1955, Collection Hirshhorn Museum and Sculpture Garden, Smithsonian Institution

## SYMMETRICAL COMPOSITION

The boundaries of a three-dimensional composition are determined by the physical edges of the created three-dimensional object. The individual parts of a three-dimensional composition are referred to as *components* or *positive spaces,* and the empty area surrounding the object is called the *negative space* (Figure 2).

In both two- and three-dimensional images, composition significantly affects the communication. In most cases, the response evoked by a completed work of art can be controlled and/or determined by the way the image has been composed. For both two- and three-dimensional images, compositions can be classified into three broad categories: symmetrical, asymmetrical, and asymmetrically symmetrical.

In symmetrical compositions, all the component parts of an image are arranged so they can be divided by or positioned equally from a central axis. The examples shown in Figure 3 are all symmetrical compositions. Each negative and positive space within the frame of reference can be divided equally by an axis (indicated by dotted lines) running through the center of the composition. This division creates two identical images (example A) or two mirror images (examples B and C). Mirror images are identical except that they are turned in opposite directions.

3

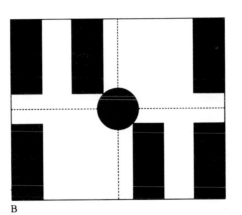

A

B

C

4

Jacques Lipchitz, *Figure*, 1926–30, Bronze, 7′1 1/4″ x 38 5/8″. The Museum of Modern Art, New York, Van Gogh Purchase Fund

Symmetrical compositions can be thought of as states of equilibrium; they constitute opposing forces—positive and negative spaces—in a state of visual balance. This characteristic of balance can be managed and controlled to obtain a desired perceptual response from the viewing audience. For example, we can visually balance an image so that it intentionally appears motionless and evoke an almost hypnotic response of power and strength. This kind of intent can be seen in the commanding sculpture by Jacques Lipschitz in Figure 4. Or, as Frank Stella's painting *Jill* (Figure 5) implies, balance can create a feeling of boredom and dullness.

As these two different examples illustrate, compositional symmetry can be used to create a wide range of responses. Symmetry can imply an unchangeable stability—a feeling of being absolute or enduring. The great pyramids of Egypt seem to evoke these responses (Figure 6). Or, as a result of its visual quality of fixed correctness, symmetry can appear rigid, cool, controlled or formal; it may seem static, steady, or monotonous. Symmetry is capable of evoking these and many other responses.

5

Frank Stella, *Jill,* 1959, enamel on canvas, 90 3/8 x 78 3/4″.
Albright-Knox Gallery,
Buffalo, New York, Gift of Seymour H. Knox, 1962

6

The Pyramids of Giza, George Holton/Photo Researchers, Inc.

7

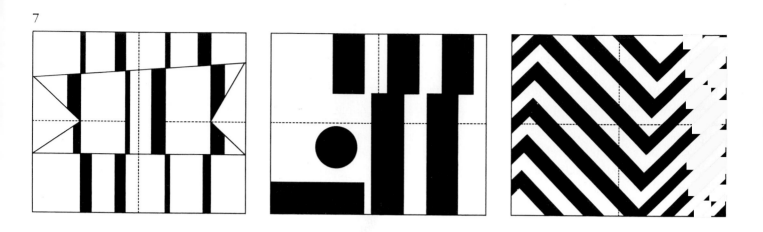

8

Tom Wesselmann, *Mouth #11*, 1967,
Dallas Museum of Fine Arts, Foundation for the Arts Collection,
Gift of the Mr. and Mrs. Edward Marcus Foundation

## ASYMMETRICAL COMPOSITION

In asymmetrical composition, all or most of the component parts of an image are arranged so they cannot be divided by, or positioned equally from, a central axis. The examples shown in Figure 7 are all asymmetrical compositions. Each of these examples is composed of parts comparable to those seen in Figure 3; however, they have been modified to make them asymmetrical rather than symmetrical images.

The visual characteristics and potential perceptual responses of asymmetry are almost directly opposite to those of symmetry. While we may see symmetrical compositions as balanced, static, or motionless, asymmetrical images can appear unbalanced. When we see a composition as visually unbalanced, we may perceive it as being unstable. This instability could be emotionally, intellectually, or even physically unsettling, as in Tom Wesselmann's *Mouth #11* (Figure 8). Similarly, Milton Glaser's illustration, *A Letter From Jail* (Figure 9), may be seen as asymmetrically disrupted. This causes visual imbalance that gives us a feeling of uneasiness. These compositional qualities reinforce the artist's intent of communicating insanity.

Like imbalance, we can use the other characteristics of asymmetry to achieve varying results. Mobility or action can be perceived as exciting, frenzied, or hectic. The characteristic of appearing dynamic can generate feelings of change, growth, or vitality. Asymmetrical composition, like symmetry, can evoke any number of responses, depending upon the artist's intent. For this reason, asymmetry is an adaptable and variable method of composing.

9

A Letter
from Jail
by
Jack
Ruby

Illustration in *Ramparts* designed by Milton Glaser

## ASYMMETRICALLY SYMMETRICAL COMPOSITION

Asymmetrically symmetrical compositions are neither strictly symmetric nor strictly asymmetric. As it suggests, asymmetrical symmetry incorporates characteristics of both symmetry and asymmetry in a single composition. This occurs when the component parts of a composition—both negative and positive spaces—are arranged in such a way that some conform to those properties associated with symmetry and others to those of asymmetry. Therefore, *asymmetrical symmetry* can be defined as a compositional arrangement in which some, but not all, component parts are divided by, or positioned equally from, a central axis (Figure 10).

Of the three broad categories of compositional types, asymmetrical symmetry probably can be seen in the greatest variety and number of visual expressions. Also, it can occur in two different forms—unintentional and intentional.

10

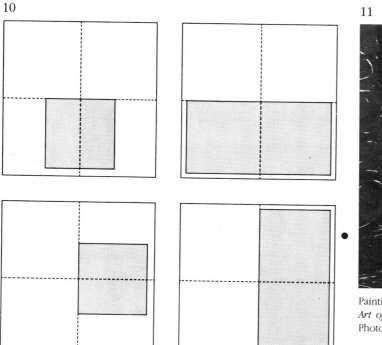

11

Painting by Eric, 5½ years old, from the exhibition, *Art of the Young Child*. December 6, 1955 through January 15, 1956. Photograph courtesy of The Museum of Modern Art, New York

## UNINTENTIONAL ASYMMETRICAL SYMMETRY

Unintentional asymmetrical symmetry is asymmetry initially conceived as symmetry; however, due to lack of technical ability, this symmetry is ultimately executed asymmetrically. An example would be an intended symmetrical composition executed without mechanical aids or measurements so the "freehand" drawing caused an unintentional result. This form of asymmetrical symmetry is often found in the visual expressions of children and primitive artists (Figures 11, 12 and 13).

Unintentional asymmetrical symmetry seems to accomplish several results simultaneously. In this type of composition, characteristics of symmetry like balance, correctness, or stability can be used to obtain their potential responses (power, strength, permanence). At the same time, enough visual variety can be introduced asymmetrically so that the image also evokes responses of human warmth, spontaneity, and so on.

12

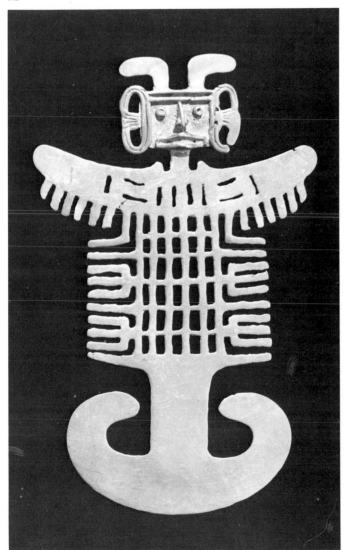

Primitive Pendant, Americas, Colombia, Tolima.
The Metropolitan Museum of Art,
The Michael C. Rockefeller Memorial Collection,
Bequest of Nelson A. Rockefeller, 1979

13

Pre-Columbian, Nyarit, Private Collection

## INTENTIONAL ASYMMETRICAL SYMMETRY

Intentional asymmetrical symmetry occurs when an artist has consciously altered a symmetrical composition. The examples in Figure 14 are asymmetrically symmetrical compositions that have been created in this way.

Intentional asymmetrical symmetry is used frequently because it can be used to emphasize any of the desired compositional properties of symmetry and/or asymmetry. With this method of composing, we can use symmetry and asymmetry in equal degrees or have one dominate the other. Any variation or combination is possible, subject only to our own desires and intent. For instance, certain properties of symmetry can be used to create a feeling of strength, along with some of the dynamic characteristics of asymmetry. The dynamic asymmetrical features do not have to be blatant, just apparent enough to enhance the symmetrical quality of power and prevent boredom.

A masterfully subtle application of this principle can be seen in the colossal statute of Ramessess II (Figure 15). In this otherwise symmetrical sculpture, one leg is brought slightly forward to introduce just enough asymmetry to give the work a dynamic quality without intruding on its visual power or presence.

It is easy for us to recognize the stable, yet dynamic, quality of unintentional asymmetrical symmetry in the art of children and primitives. Some artists study such unintentional compositions and then use intentional methods to achieve similar results. For example, Frank Cheatham's painting *Coahuila* (Figure 16) was consciously composed in this way. He intentionally used asymmetrical symmetry to achieve the emotional quality inherent in many of the visual expressions of the pre-Columbian and folk artists of Mexico.

15

Luxor Temple, Egypt (Ramessess II), Carl Frank/Photo Researchers, Inc.

14

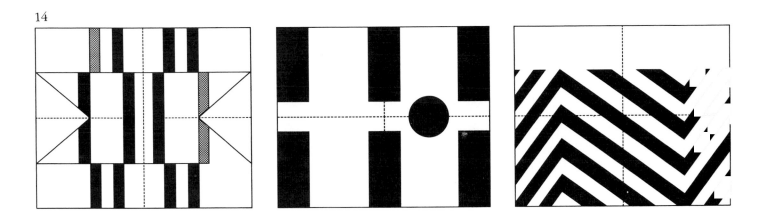

16

Frank Cheatham, *Coahuila,* 1970, Acrylic on canvas, 8 x 10′.

## FOCAL POINTS AND ACCENTS

In visual application, focal points and accents are used to direct and/or attract the eye. *Focal points* are those portions of a composition that an artist wants specifically noticed. *Accents* are relatively small areas of emphasis and are used primarily to create interest and visual variety. The use of focal points and accents can be compared to the use of spices in foods. Spices need not be used in all foods, just as focal points and accents are not always necessary in art. However, the judicious use of focal points and accents can enhance visual expressions by giving them a visibly richer flavor.

Focal points and accents are achieved basically by creating conditions of contrast. That is, they may be bigger or darker, smaller or lighter than the other compositional elements. The painting *Lighthouse Hill* by the American artist Edward Hopper (Figure 17) contains two focal points and a variety of accents. We can easily identify the two focal points as the house and the lighthouse. These focal points were created through the use of extreme value contrast on the forms. Additionally, both forms—especially the lighthouse—seem to generate a dramatic vertical thrust in contrast to a predominantly horizontal composition. The accents were also accomplished through the use of value and color contrast. They are the horizontal light values occurring in the dark hill, the glow of the sun in the upper left, and projections, recesses and details on the house and lighthouse. The placement and direction of the focal points and accents help to reinforce the spacious and haunting quality in this painting. As this example shows, focal points and accents can be used as subtle, yet compeling, compositional devices.

Edward Hopper, *Lighthouse Hill,* 1927,
Dallas Museum of Fine Arts, Gift of Mr. and Mrs. Maurice Purnell

# SECTION ONE

# 3

SHAPE AND VOLUME

In the visual arts, a *shape* is considered to be an area defined by boundaries that separate it from other areas and/or its surroundings. Ordinarily, the word "shape" is used to describe two-dimensional visual components. When referring to three-dimensional mass or volume, we substitute the word "form". For every three-dimensional volume there exists a corresponding two-dimensional shape that is its counterpart. That is, a cube is the three-dimensional equivalent of a two-dimensional square, a sphere is the three-dimensional equivalent of a two-dimensional circle, and so on. And since all two-dimensional shapes have direct visual equivalents in three-dimensional volumes, it is possible for us to establish categories for general types of shape and volume. We can do this by placing each shape and its equivalent volume in a single category that describes them both.

For easy understanding, in this chapter we have established broad categories to encompass related shapes and volumes that share common characteristics. A general term has been used to distinguish one category from another. Illustrations have been provided to show the possible two- and three-dimensional applications of each category. The first three categories of shape and volume all have their roots in geometry, the mathematical science of precise shapes and volumes.

1

2

Polychrome painted aryballus ornamented with birds and geometric ornamentation. Inca, Peru. Late post-classic period. Kemper Collection, Courtesy The Hamlyn Group

## SIMPLE GEOMETRIC

Simple geometric shape and volume is composed of basic geometric shapes and volumes that are not in combination with one another. This classification contains squares, circles, triangles—any pure shape and volume that can be constructed geometrically (Figure 1).

Simple geometric shape and volume has been used in the visual arts in a countless variety of ways. For example, on the pre-Columbian water jar (Figure 2), simple geometric shapes have been used to decorate its surface. In the three dark bands, squares have been turned on end to create diamond shapes; and in the adjacent light bands, rectangular shapes have been used to add to the overall decoration.

Another way to use shape can be seen in a painting by Jim Dine, *Self-Portrait Next To A Colored Window* (Figure 3). This work of art uses simple geometric shapes as most of its subject matter. Similarly, *Untitled* by Robert Morris (Figure 4) is an example of nonobjective sculpture in which a simple geometric volume has been employed to create a visual expression.

And, finally, the package designed for Ciba Pharmaceutical Company (Figure 5) uses simple geometric shapes to create a clean, orderly effect.

3

4

5

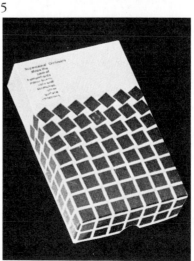

Jim Dine, *Self-Portrait Next To A Colored Window,* 1964, Dallas Museum of Fine Arts, Dallas Art Association Purchase

Robert Morris, *Untitled,* 1965–66, Dallas Museum of Fine Arts, purchased with a grant from the National Endowment for the Arts and matching funds

Physician sample mailing box designed by Aron & Falcone for Ciba Pharmaceutical Co.

## COMPLEX GEOMETRIC:
## RECTILINEAR AND CURVILINEAR

Complex geometric shapes and volumes are created by combining two or more simple shapes or volumes. Depending on the combination, these shapes and volumes can be classified in one of two categories— rectilinear or curvilinear.

### Rectilinear

The first of these two—*complex geometric rectilinear,* or simply *rectilinear*—is created by combining simple geometric shapes or volumes that result in straight line and surface configurations. They do not possess any lines and surfaces that are curved (Figure 6).

Rectilinear shapes and volumes, like simple geometric ones, are used frequently and effectively in the visual arts. An example of the use of a variety of re-

ctilinear shapes can be seen in *Color Perspective* by Jacques Villon (Figure 7). Another example is Figure 8, *Smoke,* by Tony Smith. This large free-standing sculpture illustrates the use of a single rectilinear volume. In addition, multiple rectilinear volumes can be assembled to form more complex structures, like the Art and Architecture Building at Yale University designed by Paul Rudolph (Figure 9). These are just a sampling of the many ways we can use rectilinear shapes and volumes in designing works of art.

6

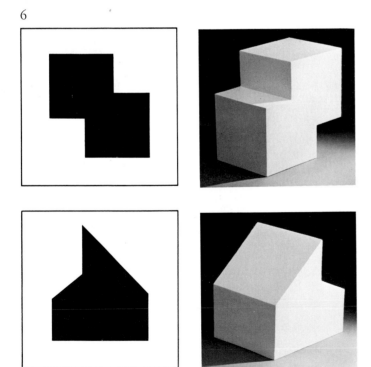

7

Jacques Villon, *Color Perspective,* 1921, The Solomon R. Guggenheim Museum Collection, New York. Gift Katherine S. Drier Estate

8

Tony Smith, *Smoke,* Courtesy The Pace Gallery, New York

9

Art and Architecture Building, Yale University
designed by Paul Rudolph.
Photograph courtesy Division of Architecture, Texas Tech University

## Curvilinear

Complex geometric shapes and volumes also can be categorized as *complex geometric curvilinear,* or *curvilinear.* These shapes and volumes are formed in the same way as the rectilinear—by combining simple geometric shapes or volumes. Unlike rectilinear, however, curvilinear shapes and volumes incorporate in their configurations curved as well as straight lines and surfaces (Figure 11).

Curvilinear shapes and volumes can be found in many forms of nature, so it seems only natural that these shapes and volumes would appear in a wide variety of works of art. One such example composed of curvilinear volumes is Antoni Gaudi's Casa Mila Apart-

10

Casa Mila (detail), Barcelona, designed by Antoni Gaudi. Photograph courtesy Division of Architecture, Texas Tech University

ment House (Figure 10); another illustration is the Alaskan shirt in Figure 12. In a third example, Hebrew letters on an invitation to a slide lecture concerning the discovery of a biblical city (Figure 13) have been treated as complex curvilinear shapes that not only communicate verbally, but create a beautiful visual expression as well.

11

12

13

Man's shirt, woven by the Tlingit Indians of Alaska,
Courtesy Museum of the American Indian, Heye Foundation, N.Y.
Photograph, Carmelo Guadagno

Invitation designed by Stan Brod for the Hebrew Union College
Jewish Institute of Religion, Cincinnati, Ohio

## ORGANIC

The fourth general category used to classify shapes and volumes is *organic*. Organic shapes and volumes are described by free-flowing curves. Like curvilinear shapes and volumes, they are also found frequently in nature—the volumes fluids naturally assume; the shapes and volumes created by forms of plant, animal or insect life (Figure 14).

In visual art forms, organic shapes and volumes frequently reflect nature. For example, the volume of the seventeenth-century flask in Figure 15 is organic, and the majority of the shapes included on its richly decorated surface were inspired by natural forms. In Figure 16, the trademark design for a plumbing manufacturer consists of two identical organic shapes designed to evoke a feeling of free-flowing fluid. And finally, a painting by Modigliani (Figure 17) exemplifies the use of very sensitive organic shapes: The woman's face, earlobe, eyes, and the overall shape of her figure are all examples of organic shape.

15

Flask. Persian 17th cen., Collection Victoria & Albert Museum, London

14

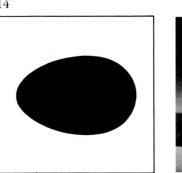

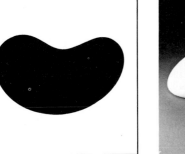

16

Trademark for Price Pfister Plumbing designed by Frank Cheatham

## ACCIDENTAL

The last general category is *accidental* shape and volume. These can be created in an unintentional, unplanned manner, or they may be the result of intentionally using a material or process that cannot be controlled completely. In using both approaches, the shapes and volumes created may be seen as accidental. For instance, if we splatter ink unintentionally on a piece of paper, the resulting shape or form will be accidental because it is unplanned. If we dropped the ink intentionally, the visual result would still be accidental because the process of spilling cannot be completely controlled. Various examples of accidental shapes and volumes are shown in Figure 18.

17

Amedeo Modigliani, *Anna Zborowska,* 1917,
Oil on canvas, 51 1/4 x 32".
Collection, The Museum of Modern Art, New York.
Lillie P. Bliss Collection

18

Accidental shapes were consciously used in Western art for the first time by the Abstract Expressionists in the early 1940s. Before that time, many Eastern artists—particularly Chinese and Japanese ceramists—used shapes intentionally created by accident of material or process. In the visual arts today, accidental shapes and volumes created intentionally are common. For instance, *Gallas Rock* by Peter Voulkos (Figure 19) is a large ceramic sculpture of combined volumes that was created primarily by accidental processes. In Figure 20, the photograph of the man was deliberately distorted so that an accidental shape was created. A third example, *Boon,* a painting by Jack Tworkov in 1960 (Figure 21), is composed entirely of negative and positive accidental shapes. These are just a few of the many ways accidental shapes are created and used for visual expression.

20

Photographer: Robert Suddarth

19

Peter Voulkos, *Gallas Rock,* 1959–60, Univ. of California, Los Angeles. Gift of Julianne Kemper

21

Jack Tworkov, *Boon,* 1960
Collection The Nancy Hoffman Gallery, New York

## CREATING SHAPE AND VOLUME

Several methods can be used by visual artists to create shape and volume, some more obvious than others. One of the obvious methods is to construct geometrically known shapes and volumes. Another is to create unknown shapes and volumes through process or media usage, as the Abstract Expressionists did.

Two less obvious methods we can use to create shapes and volumes are those of addition and subtraction. Shapes and volumes designed in these two ways are the result of conscious visual exploration and application of esthetic judgment.

To arrive at a shape or volume by addition, a group of previously determined shapes and volumes are first selected. These are then combined and recombined in a variety of ways until a new shape or volume is created that is satisfactory. Figure 22 shows a sequence of new volumes being created from previously existing ones. These have been formed by adding various volumes in a number of combinations.

Arriving at shape or volume by subtraction involves starting with a single known shape or volume and subtracting component parts until a desired shape or volume is created. Figure 23 shows a geometric shape that has had component parts subtracted in a progressive sequence, from left to right, from the original configuration.

22

23

# SECTION ONE

# 4

SPACE

Any form or shape can be perceived as existing in and occupying space. In the absence of a form or shape, a sense of emptiness, or empty space, occurs. Generally, then, *space* can be defined as the distance, interval or area between, around, or within things. When using space in the visual arts, we define it more specifically as the actual or illusory distance, interval, or area that is between, around, or within the components of a visual expression. All visual expressions incorporate *flat, illusory,* or *actual* space—either individually or in a variety of combinations.

1

Flat stamp from Veracruz, Courtesy
Dover Publications, Inc.,
*Design Motifs of Ancient Mexico* by Jorge Enciso

2

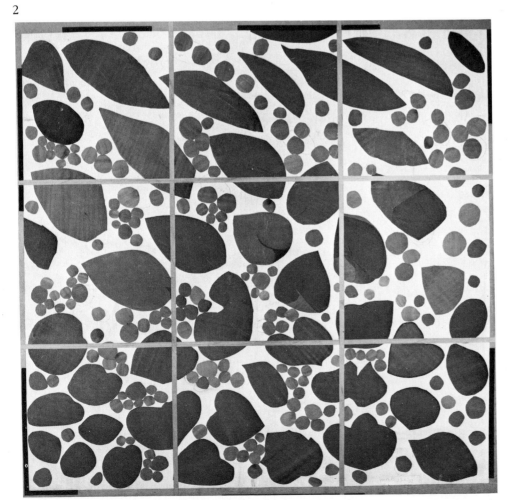

Henri Matisse, *Ivy in Flower,* 1953. Dallas Museum of Fine Arts, Foundation for the Arts Collection.
Gift of the Albert and Mary Lasker Foundation, New York

3

Student project:
bookcover designed by Terri Black

## FLAT SPACE

Flat space consists of two dimensions—height and width—and lends itself easily to use in two-dimensional works. Since flat space is two-dimensional, there is usually little or no illusion of depth. The resulting images are direct and appear to lay flat against the surface.

Artists for centuries have used flat space representationally and abstractly to express their ideas. An imaginative example of the latter can be seen in the stylized rattlesnake image made by a pre-Columbian artist's clay stamp (Figure 1). No attempt was made to create the illusion of the snake's volume or the space in which it existed. Instead, the artist's concern seems to have been the re-creation of characteristic features that would communicate "rattlesnake," rather than the space it occupied.

Similarly, Henri Matisse utilized abstract flat space in some of his most sophisticated works. For instance, in *Ivy in Flower* (Figure 2) it can be seen that all the leaf shapes appear to exist on one plane; these shapes have no dimension of depth since they were executed as silhouette shapes out of cut paper. As a result, the final arrangement appears flat both in space and in imagery.

Flat space can be dramatic and direct in its simplicity. For example, a book cover designed by Terri Black (Figure 3) has utilized flat space and flat curvilinear shapes to communicate the content of the book's text.

Jean Dubuffet provides a clear example of the use of flat space in his work *Business Prospers* (Figure 4). In this piece, Dubuffet presents the intriguing image of a city that appears to have been flattened by a giant steamroller. As a result, the image seems to be affixed to a flat surface.

4

Jean Dubuffet, *Business Prospers,* 1961, 65 x 86 5/8". The Museum of Modern Art, New York. Mrs. Simon Guggenheim Fund

## FLAT FLUCTUATING SPACE

Flat space that has been divided into approximately equal proportions of figure and ground has a tendency to create visual ambiguity. In such compositions, it is difficult to determine which portion is figure and which is ground. The relationship between the two continually fluctuates—a portion initially perceived as figure can, in the next moment, appear to be ground, and then just as quickly, figure again. An example of such a figure-ground ambiguity can be seen in Figure 5. This composition appears continually to fluctuate. It can be read first as white lines on a black background, then as black lines on a white ground. As a result, an illusion of depth or space is created even though all the components of the composition are spatially flat.

Because of its spatial potential, we can use alternating figure-ground relationships to dramatize flat space. An example of this can be seen in a pre-Columbian design motif (Figure 6). The illusion created by fluctuating space acts as a dimensional contrast to the flat walls of the architecture to which the design was once applied.

Although both of the previous examples seem to be divided mathematically into equal proportions, this is not mandatory. *D-P Diagonal* (Figure 7) by Norman Ives is an example of illusory fluctuating space that has visually—rather than mathematically—divided figure and ground into equal proportions. In Figure 8, a contemporary trademark design for a Swiss process engraving company illustrates an equal *visual* division of figure and ground that has in fact been approximated. The stylization of a printing dot pattern has created fluctuating positive-negative space that gives this trademark both visual and conceptual strength.

5

6

Pre-Columbian design motif, Courtesy Dover Publications, Inc., *Design Motifs of Ancient Mexico* by Jorge Enciso

Trademark designed by Gerstner, Gredinger & Kutter for Schwitter Ltd, Basle, a process engraving firm.

8

7

Norman Ives, *D-P Diagonal,* 1964. Collection Mr. Malcolm Grear, Providence, Rhode Island

## ILLUSORY SPACE

Illusory space—the illusion of space—is used frequently in two-dimensional expressions and, with less frequency, in three-dimensional work. In a two-dimensional work, a piece of canvas or paper is seen primarily as a flat surface until an image is created on it. Often we can perceive this created image as a solid shape or form occupying space, and the area that does not contain the imagery is seen as unoccupied, surrounding space. Because this sensation is perceptual rather than actual, the space created is an illusion.

With illusory space, we can adjust and vary the degrees of distance or depth so they are perceived in different ways. For discussion, we can group these variations into three categories: *shallow, moderate* and *deep/infinite* space.

## Shallow Space

Flat space has already been described as having height, width and, occasionally, accidental depth or surrounding space in which fluctuation can occur. Shallow space may be defined as space that seems to exist in and around shapes to a very limited degree. An example of this can be seen in Figure 9. The placement of the lighter typographic elements over the darker ones creates the illusion that they exist on a plane located slightly in front of the others.

In creating shallow space, it is not always necessary for the imagery to be completely flat; it is possible for the image to imply space by creating an illusion of volume or depth. In the page from a booklet (Figure 10) space is created through the suggestion of the volume of a group of pencils. Since the actual circumference and depth of pencils is known to be small, the space they occupy can be seen as shallow.

9

Student project: bookcover design by Tracy Hart

10

Student project, page from a booklet by Alan Colvin

## Moderate Space

The perception of moderate space is more subjective than that of flat or shallow space. It can be loosely defined as that space in and around shapes not limited enough to be flat or shallow space, but not so expanded to be deep or infinite; moderate space exists between these extremes.

An excellent example of moderate space is found in Lawrence Drieband's painting (Figure 11). In this work, the illusion of depth results from the volume of both the figure and the chair. Most of us have experienced the approximate dimensions and volume of an easy chair. In this case, moderate space can be perceived as a result of prior knowledge.

John Clem Clarke's untitled painting (Figure 12) also illustrates moderate space. The staging of light and the density of the surrounding objects implies that the figures are in a secluded, rather than an open, space. The scale of the figures also suggests that they are very close to us. In view of this, it can be felt that the space around the figures is rather intimate, since the artist has dealt with moderate space.

11

Laurence Dreiband, *Rainbow,* 1969, Collection of the artist

12

John Clem Clarke, *Untitled,* 1970. Courtesy OK Harris Works of Art, New York

### Deep/Infinite Space

Deep/infinite space implies great distances in and around the image being presented. It appears to extend far beyond, in front of, or to the sides of shapes within a composition. It can also be perceived as extending into or beyond the picture plane into infinity.

In contrast to John Clem Clarke's painting, Harold Bruder's *Canyon Encounter* (Figure 13) is spatially wide open and a good example of deep/infinite space. The plane of the mountain meadow seems to extend beyond both sides of the picture plane. Similarly, the depth of the canyon floor appears to reach far behind the figures, winding its way around and through the steep façades of the canyon walls for a long and indeterminate distance. The illusion of deep space is reinforced by the posture and attitude of the figures, since the woman on the right appears to be gazing into the deep space she is experiencing. Finally, the sky creates a feeling of vastness that completes this work's effective illusion of deep/infinite space.

In a similar way, deep/infinite space plays an important role in James Howze's fine drawing (Figure 14). The converging lines in the ground plane seem to extend back into infinity. Also, this feeling of infinite space is reinforced by the artist's depiction of flight. The winged figure appears to be moving toward the viewer and the airplane seems to be flying in a direction to the left. Additionally, since the wing on the right overlaps the perimeter of the picture plane, the winged figure seems to be flying through space beyond the drawing itself.

13

Harold Bruder, *Canyon Encounter,* Collection Mr. and Mrs. Donald B. Straus

James Howze, *Lysander Over Anvil Bay,* 1974. Collection of the artist

15

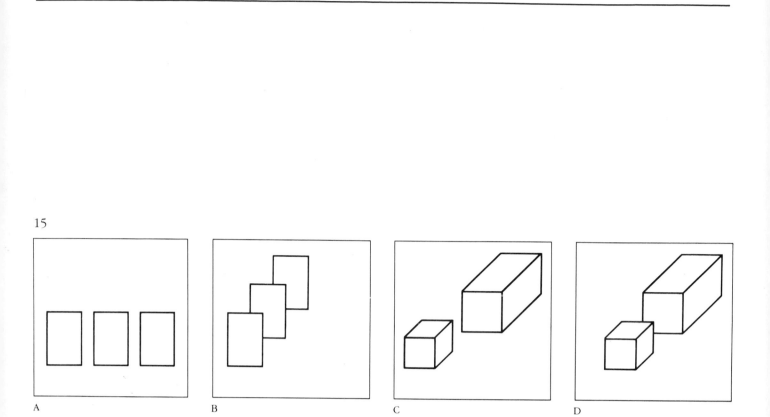

A    B    C    D

16

Paul Klee, *Fugue in Red,* ©1981, Copyright by COSMOPRESS, Geneva & ADAGP, Paris

## ILLUSORY SPACE TECHNIQUES

There are many means and methods by which we can create spatial effects; and for maximum effect, these spatial techniques are frequently combined and used simultaneously. For easier understanding, however, they are discussed individually here. The following are some of the basic techniques for creating illusory space.

### Overlapping

Since we know that two objects cannot occupy the same space simultaneously, it is possible to create an illusion of depth simply by overlapping shapes. In Figure 15(a), for instance, the shapes exist separately and the space appears flat. However, in Figure 15(b) the shapes have been overlapped so they appear to be behind one another and to recede into the picture plane, creating the illusion of depth. In Figure 15(c), an illusion of space is achieved because the separate figures appear to have volume, and volume automatically implies depth. As a result, when the volumetric figures are overlapped in Figure 15(d), the illusion and degree of

depth is even more pronounced and dramatic than in Figures 15(b) or 15(c).

In Paul Klee's *Fugue in Red* (Figure 16), smaller flat shapes have been placed in front of larger ones to create shallow space by overlapping.

In contrast, Henri Rousseau's painting *The Sleeping Gypsy* (Figure 17) illustrates the illusion of deep space achieved through overlapping. The reclining figure overlaps the form of the lion to suggest that it is in front of the lion. The figure's right shoulder also overlaps the ground to imply that this surface has depth as well as width. In addition, the illusion of great distance has been created because the mountains appear to exist behind the form of the lion. Since mountains are known to be generally larger than lions, it is logical that they must be far away to seem so comparatively small. Finally, the overlapping of the land masses themselves creates an illusion of deep, unknown distance.

17

Henri Rousseau, *The Sleeping Gypsy,* 1897, Oil on canvas, 51″ x 6′7″.
Collection, The Museum of Modern Art, New York. Gift of Mrs. Simon Guggenheim

## Perspective

In creating the illusion of space, linear perspective can give the illusion of volume and the spatial distance existing between and around volumetric forms. As a result, space is implied when volume is implied. We can effectively create this type of spatial illusion mechanically or spontaneously.

*Perspective* can be defined as a method for presenting objects so that their representation corresponds in distance and depth to what appears to the eye. When using perspective, particular attention is paid to how an object "appears" to the eye, rather than to what we know experientially or intellectually about its actual physical properties. For instance, although we know that a box has a top, bottom, and four sides, when we look at it, three of these six planes are the most we can possibly see. And in some instances our point of view makes it impossible for more than one or two of these planes to be visible to us (Figure 18). Therefore, when we are presenting an illusion of the volume of a box, our initial concern is re-creating how it appears visually, not how it is physically.

In representing objects as they appear, the point of view of the observer—or the *station point*—must be taken into account. For instance, if an object is far away from the station point it will appear smaller than if it is close; if an object is very close to the station point, it may not be visible in its entirety to the viewer. These two situations can be experienced simply by holding our hand first at arm's length and then close to the face. At arm's length, the hand appears to be a certain size, and all of it can be seen. When we place the hand close to the face, it will appear comparatively larger, and only a portion of it will be visible. In reality, the size and shape of the hand have not changed. This example demonstrates how the relative distance of an object from the station point can determine the appearance of its size and shape.

In addition to the station point, the *eye level* of the observer is an important consideration when recreating the appearance of objects. For instance, if we place a box on a surface below the level of our eyes, only the top and two sides of the box will be visible. In this case, the eye level is said to be high. In comparison, if a box is at a level higher than our eyes, only the bottom and two of its sides will be seen. This situation is called low eye level. If neither the top nor the bottom of the box is visible, then it is existing on a plane even with our eyes, or at exact eye level (Figure 19).

Like station point and eye level, the directional angle of tilt of the horizontal edges of a form is essential to representing objects through the use of perspective. Take, for example, viewing a tall building. When we look up at a tall building, the upper edges will appear to tilt in a downward direction; when looking down at the ground plane, the lower edges will appear to slant upward. The appearance of tilting edges can be seen in Charles Sheeler's *City Interior* (Figure 20). In this painting, the bottom edge of the large building on the left has been slanted in an upward direction, while the top and bottom edges of the windows have been tilted down. Even though buildings and windows do not physically tilt up and down, Sheeler has represented them this way because that is how they would appear to the human eye when viewed from a particular station point and eye level. In addition, the use of a rather mechanical perspective in this expression is appropriate because it emphasizes the mechanical look and feel of certain urban conditions.

18

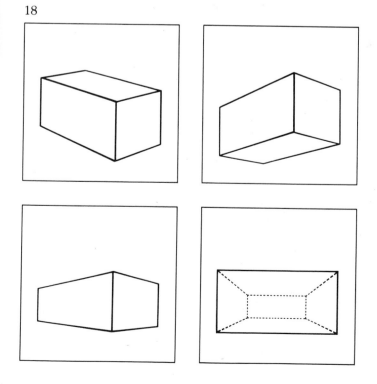

19

High Eye Level

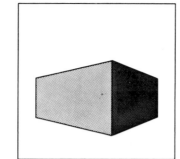

Eye Level

Low Eye Level

20

Charles Sheeler, *City Interior,* 1936, aqueous adhesive and oil on composition board, 22 1/8 x 26 15/16".
Worcester Art Museum, Bequest of Elizabeth M. Sawyer, in memory of Jonathan and Elizabeth M. Sawyer

In comparison, the British artist Anthony Green has altered perspective to create a different spatial illusion. In his painting *The Red Chair* (Figure 21), space is suggested by tilting the edges of the objects on the ground plane in an upward direction. In addition, an unusual effect is achieved because he breaks one of the rules of perspective—only one eye level can exist in a single view. However, in this work the artist has used multiple eye levels. There is a feeling of looking down at the ground plane (rugs, box, tray) while simultaneously looking directly at the woman and chair. This illusion is created by using several high eye levels for the ground plane and an exact eye level for the seated figure. In this way, Green has produced an unexpected visual situation that is exciting and dynamic without destroying the illusion of space.

## Isometric Planes

Perspective has been described as a two-dimensional representation of images as they appear to the eye, and one of its features is the tilting of the horizontal edges of planes. When the edges of tilted horizontal planes are extended, they will eventually converge and the overall surface area of the planes will be diminished (Figure 22).

Isometric planes, in comparison to perspective, are not used to attempt to re-create objects as they appear to the eye. And although volume and depth are implied, the edges of isometric planes never converge because all the sets of parallel lines remain intentionally equidistant. Specifically, then, *isometric planes* can be defined as the component parts of a drawn figure indicating three dimensions, but not in perspective.

The volumetric and spatial differences of perspective and isometric planes can be seen in Figure 23. In this simple example, the isometric figures appear to recede upward and backward on a tilted surface so that the space created is rather shallow. In comparison, the figures in perspective appear to be on a flat surface and their planes recede directly back into the picture plane to create a space deeper than that implied by the isometric drawing.

It can be seen in Figure 23 that each plane of the isometric figures presents more overall surface area than those of the perspective figures. For this reason, isometric figures can be more useful than perspective figures when it is necessary to communicate a large amount of information about a plane or figure. A diagram representing an architectural framing detail (Figure 24) effectively utilizes the available surface space created by isometric planes. The isometric planes have provided the needed space to communicate precise information concerning the type of joints used for particu-

Anthony Green, *The Red Chair,* 1970. Collection Rowan Gallery, London

lar structural members. Another reason for creating an isometric diagram can be the direct result of limited actual space. To communicate large amounts or complex information on a small amount of available surface space—like the page of a book or manual—it may be necessary to use depth as a substitute for length or width. Isometric planes are ideal for solving this type of space problem.

The fluctuating optical illusion created in a handsome silk and satin quilt (Figure 25) is also made possible by the use of isometric planes. When we view the quilt one way, the dark planes appear to be the bottoms of boxlike forms. When viewed another way, they become the tops. The use of isometric planes has created a continually changing and exciting pattern.

22

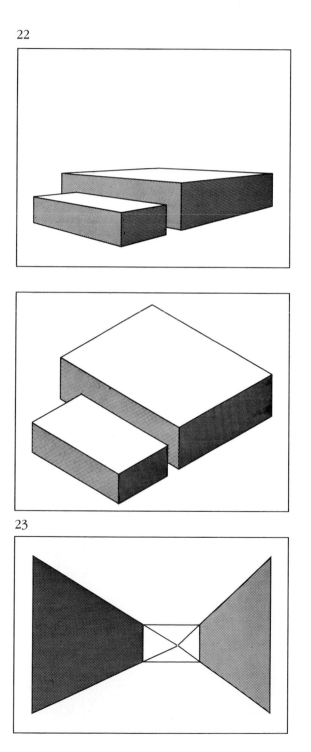

23

24

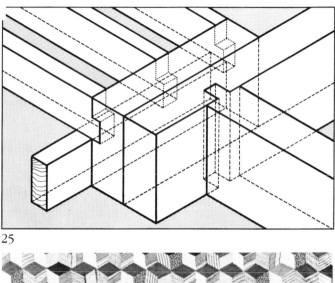

25

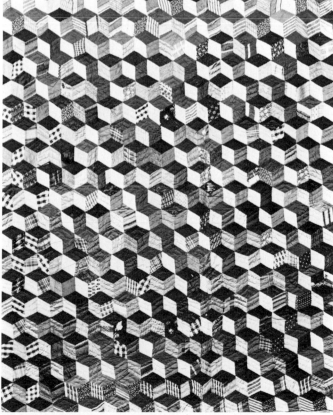

Silk Box Quilt, American, c. 1860. The Brooklyn Museum, presented in memory of Mrs. Charles M. Davidson

### Foreground, Middleground, and Background

Another way we can achieve the illusion of space is through the creation of foreground, middleground, and background. In some ways, this spatial method functions like perspective, since there is a concern with the position of the viewer. Foreground, for instance, can be defined as the portion of a picture that appears nearest us, and background as the farthest. The area in the picture between the foreground and the background is called middleground. Figure 26 illustrates this spatial concept.

The creation of a foreground, middleground, and background is primarily responsible for the illusion of

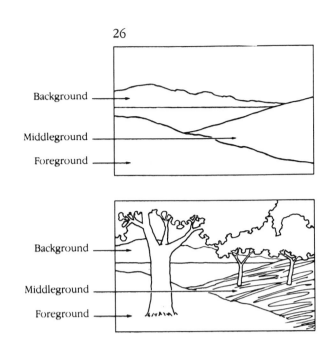

27. Pierre Bonnard, *Dining Room in The Country,* 1913. Collection Minneapolis Institute of Arts

moderate and deep space in Pierre Bonnard's painting *Dining Room in the Country* (Figure 27). Since the closest objects in the picture to us are the table, chairs, and window on the right, they can be considered the foreground. The middleground consists of the wall on the right, the door and doorway, and the leaning figure at the right. The farthest portion from us—the background—is the area beyond the interior containing the garden, tree, and additional shrubbery.

While this spatial method is most often associated with perspective, it can also be seen in works in which perspective is not used, such as Vasily Kandinsky's *Improvisation 30 (Cannon)* (Figure 28). The use of foreground (cannon and smoke shapes moving from right to left), middleground (center shapes moving to upper right), and background (road behind the cannon winding to the left behind the middleground shapes) has created an effective illusion of deep space.

## Atmospheric Perspective

Since the value of objects changes with relative distance, varying the value within the imagery can create illusions of space and depth. This method for creating the illusion of space and volume is called *atmospheric,* or *aerial,* perspective. For example, an object that is far away from us may appear to be lighter in value than when it is close because of the amount of distance or atmosphere that exists between us and the object. Also, far distances cause our eyes to perceive the acute edges of objects as being diffused.

The use of atmoshperic perspective can be found in Robert Rauschenberg's *Estate* (Figure 29). The roughly defined vertical, light value shape in the center of the painting appears to recede into the picture plane, while below it and to the right the clearly defined dark shapes seem to advance.

28

Wassily Kandinsky, *Improvisation No. 30 (Warlike Theme),* 1913, oil on canvas, 43 1/4 x 43 3/4".
Arthur Jerome Eddy Memorial Collection, Collection of The Art Institute of Chicago

29

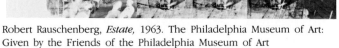

Robert Rauschenberg, *Estate,* 1963. The Philadelphia Museum of Art: Given by the Friends of the Philadelphia Museum of Art

Usually, lighter values appear to recede, while darker values come forward. However, the extreme values of black and white can be an exception. They have the ability to advance or to recede depending on their size, placement, and amount in a composition. For instance, look at the two areas of white in Paul Klee's *Before the Gates of Kairouan* (Figure 30); a small white domelike shape near the top appears to be far away due to its placement and size. Conversely, because of its positioning and size, a large white area at the extreme left of the painting seems to exist in the foreground. In addition, subtle value variations and indistinct edges of shapes create an atmospheric perspective that suggests the city is mysterious and ethereal.

## Rendering

Rendering can be defined as the two-dimensional visual presentation of a form as it might appear in three dimensions. And since volume can be indicated by this process, rendering may be considered an indirect method for creating the illusion of space.

Like perspective, rendering is primarily based on how things appear to the eye, as well as how things appear in relation to one or more sources of light. In Figure 31, the first form is created by line and perspective only to indicate those features that communicate volume—height, width, and depth. Although this form has illusory volume, little substance has been implied, since no light source is taken into account. In comparison, the second form appears to have not only volume, but some substance as well, because partial rendering has been used to create value variations of shade and shadow—conditions that automatically imply light. This

30

Paul Klee, *Before the Gates of Kairouan,* (c)1981, Copyright by COSMOPRESS, Geneva & ADAGP, Paris

form suggests only a minimum amount of substance, though, because the lines initially used to delineate it are still apparent and operative. The third form has the illusion of volume and substance as a result of fully rendered shades and shadows. Also, because the human eye does not actually see "line-drawn" objects, but rather value changes that define their edges, the use of line has been avoided in the final expression. The combination of full shade and shadow and the absence of line gives this form maximum substance.

Besides being visually intriguing, rendering appeals to the sense of touch. A fully rendered image may create an illusion of mass and volume so convincing that we may have the desire to touch or handle the image. Such is the case in William Harnett's painting *Munich Still Life* (Figure 33). Rendered light, shade, and shadows have been used to create the illusion of volumetric forms and their various textures. In addition, the use of rendering as a communication tool, rather than just an illusionary technique, has assisted in effectively conveying a feeling of warmth and intimacy.

In Jane Cheatham's *Bedroom Drawing* (Figure 32), a dramatic illusion of volume and space has been created. Carefully rendered changes in value communicate soft forms and silken surfaces. Also, shadows cast on the forms to the left suggest the existence of a light source and objects that are beyond the immediate picture plane.

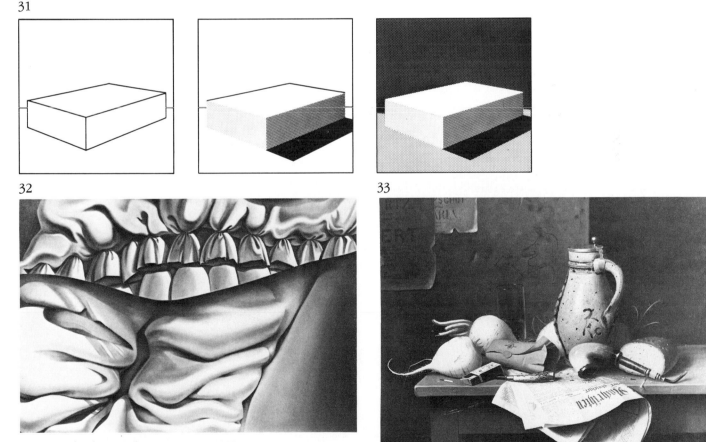

31

32

Jane Hart Cheatham, *Bedroom Drawing,* 1977

33

William Michael Harnett, *Munich Still Life,* 1882. Collection Dallas Museum of Fine Arts, Dallas Art Association Purchase

## ACTUAL SPACE

Whereas two-dimensional illusory space can only suggest three dimensions, actual space *is* three-dimensional. Like illusory space, actual space can be manipulated to create different types of space—shallow, moderate, and deep/infinite. When we produce each of these in actual space, it is directly related to the size or scale of volumetric objects that exist in the space; it is also specifically defined by surrounding volumes.

With actual space we also have the potential to create strong emotional and intellectual responses. For example, in Marcel Duchamp's small sculpture, *Why Not Sneeze Rose Selavy?* (Figure 34), use of actual space emotionally communicates intimacy and confinement. In this expression, the space is defined by the rectangular planes that surround it, as well as the contained forms of the thermometer and sugar cubes. Also, since the size of these objects is small, the actual space created seems shallow.

In contrast, the interior courtyard of the Ford Foundation Building designed by Kevin Roche (Figure 35) creates a space that is vertically deep. This space is defined by its surrounding planes as well as the scale relationship of the height of the building to the size of the human figures that use the space. This relationship emphasizes the deep space of the courtyard.

In Philip Johnson's interior of the Munson-Williams-Proctor Institute (Figure 36), deep space that is horizontal rather than vertical can be seen. And, as in Roche's courtyard, the relative size of the human form to the overall space reinforces the feeling of dramatic depth.

34

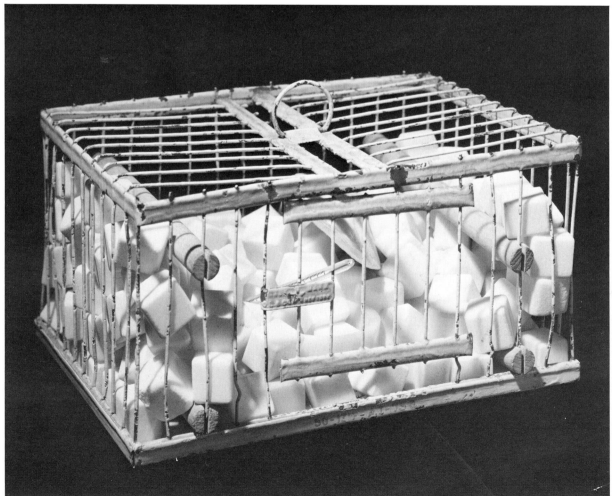

Marcel Duchamp, *Ready-Made, Why Not Sneeze Rose Selavy?,* 1921.
Philadelphia Museum of Art, The Louise and Walter Arensberg Collection

## Special Considerations

Actual space is used in sculpture, architecture, ceramics, weaving, jewelry, industrial design, product design, and so on. In all these disciplines, actual space—like two-dimensional flat and illusory space—must deal with elements such as composition, unity, shape, size, volume. However, the inclusion of a third dimension—depth—creates concerns that are not always present with two-dimensional representations.

The first of these concerns is *all around space*. Unlike two-dimensional works which are viewed only from the front, three-dimensional expressions are seen from all sides. Since we can observe such works of art from any point, visual interest is usually created around the entire expression.

*Touch* is another concern of actual space. Since even two-dimensional rendered forms appeal to the sense of touch, it is understandable that actual three-dimensional objects have an even greater potential for sensory appeal. For instance, Brancusi's *Sculpture for the Blind* (Figure 37) is meant to be touched. The visual purity of the form is intriguing and beautiful, but its tactile, sensory quality communicates most effectively Brancusi's intent.

36. Interior, Munson-Williams-Proctor Institute by Philip Johnson

35

Interior Courtyard, Ford Foundation Building by Kevin Roche. Photograph, Ezra Stoller, Copyright ESTO

37

Constantin Brancusi, *Sculpture for the Blind,* 1916. Philadelphia Museum of Art, The Louise and Walter Arensberg Collection

The sense of *sound* is also a frequent consideration in three-dimensional works. Many fountains, for example, have running water that produces sound. The flow and amount of the water must be controlled so that its sound reinforces, rather than contradicts, the intended content of the fountain. If a sculptural fountain is intended to give peace and comfort, it would not be designed with a loud, annoying gush of running water. The sound of water can become an integral part of actual space. It can be used to reinforce the content of three-dimensional expressions like Louis Kahn's fountain treatment for the Kimbell Art Museum in Fort Worth, Texas (Figure 38). In addition, sound is essential to architecture. The acoustics of a space are directly related to its height, width, and depth—more simply, it is the way an actual space sounds.

40

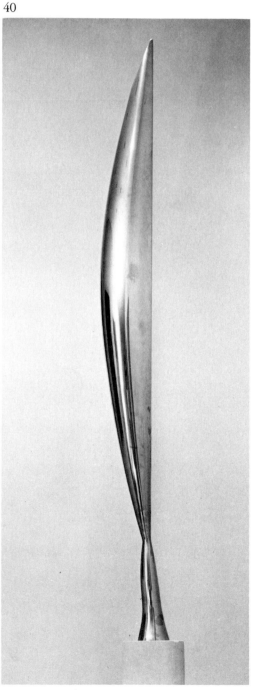

38

The Kimbell Museum, Fort Worth, Texas by Louis Kahn.
Photograph, Elizabeth Skidmore Sasser

Constantin Brancusi, *Bird in Space,* 1925.
Collection Mr. & Mrs. William A.M. Burden, N.Y.

Finally, the matter of available *light*—natural or artificial—is often critical to actual space. Three-dimensional works that are thoughtfully and carefully lighted can be visually dramatic (Figure 39). The relationship of light and form is important in expressing the content of Constantin Brancusi's *Bird in Space* (Figure 40). The reflection of light on the mirrorlike surface of this sculpture reinforces its concept of motion. The light is as much a part of the sculptural material as the chrome.

Shade and shadow patterns created by natural light can be emotionally intriguing, as in André Bloc's garden space in France (Figure 41). When sunlight filters through the organic forms that define the space, changing patterns are created in much the same way as those created by sunlight filtering through a grove of trees. For this reason, the presence of light is essential for the emotional content of this space.

39

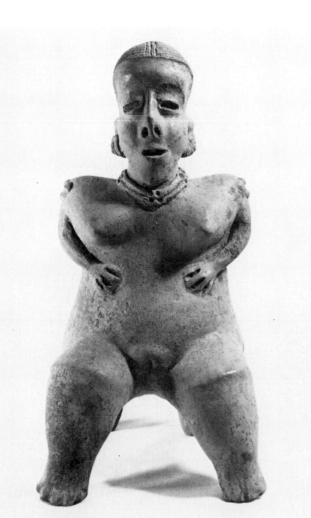

Pre-Columbian, Colima. Private Collection

41

Sculpturally Conceived House by Andre Bloc. Collection of the artist, Meudon, France. Courtesy Leni Iselin, Paris

## Environmental Concerns

The environment—flora, fauna, sun, temperature, wind, rain—can play an important role in the planning and placement of architecture and sculpture. In some cases, the environment is completely inseparable from the expression, as in Robert Smithson's *Amarillo Ramp* (Figure 42). In a similar way, the massive forms at Stonehenge (Figure 43) are related to the environment—theoretically in ground placement and positioning in relation to the stars. Though the exact nature of this relationship has been an unsolved mystery for centuries, it nevertheless communicates awesome actual space and volume.

Respect for and response to the environment has long been an important—and controversial—issue in the history of architectural design. Some architects feel that an architectural form should stand apart from the environment and assert itself. Others feel a form should have an affinity for its specific environment and grow out of it like an outcropping of rocks. Consideration of these viewpoints—as well as those previously mentioned in relation to the environment—indicates how important environmental concerns can be to the creation of actual space and volume.

42

Robert Smithson, *Amarillo Ramp*. Courtesy Stanley Marsh

43

Stonehenge. Photograph, Robert Perl

# SECTION ONE

5

CONTRAST

1

Abu-Simbel, The Colossi of Ramesses II. George Holton/Photo Researchers, Inc.

In the visual arts, *contrast* can be defined as the creation of visual opposition by diverse treatment of component parts of a gestalt. Basically, the use of contrast serves two purposes: It introduces visual variety into an expression, and it heightens the overall visual effect. It is used frequently in both two- and three-dimensional works to strengthen visual statements and to reinforce communication.

The differences created by contrast can make a visual statement more dramatic and exciting. The more striking and emphatic the visual differences are, the more engaging and interesting the overall expression can be. This is true as long as the visual contrasts used in a single expression are not too disparate, or their number too great. In either of these situations—too great a number or too great a difference—the overall effect could be weakened, rather than strengthened, by contrast. Therefore, like a tightrope walker, the artist must attempt to achieve a balance. With the proper balance of number and kind, artists can create a stimulating, effective visual statement.

To achieve this kind of visual success, we can contrast a large variety and number of visual properties and characteristics either individually or in any number of combinations and variations. The first of these is contrast of scale.

## CONTRAST OF SCALE

We often use the term *scale* to describe size. "Large scale" indicates that something is large in size; "small scale" implies that something is small in size. Usually, this classification according to size is determined by relative comparisons. For example, if a whale is compared to a human, it may appear enormous in size. However, when the same whale is compared to an ocean liner, it might be considered rather small. Furthermore, we have a tendency to make such size comparisons based on a relationship to human scale: Objects are regarded as large or small according to their relationship to the size of the human figure.

Ultimately, these relationships of comparative size can have a significant effect on human response. Objects that are considerably larger than we are appear uncontrollable, overwhelming, awesome, or threatening; things that are much smaller may seem fragile, precious, or intimate. As a result of these inherent qualities, we can use both large and small scale to provoke any number of varying responses.

Contrast of scale has been used by artists for centuries. The artists who created Abu Simbel (Figure 1) used colossal scale—each figure is over 65 feet in height—to communicate the awesome power of Ramesses II. Three-dimensional expressions of this type make obvious use of contrast of size relative to human proportion because we are able to make direct physical comparisons between the object and ourselves.

Although it is not quite so obvious, artists working two-dimensionally also use scale—both large and small—relative to human proportions. One method of achieving two-dimensional contrast of scale is by direct comparison of the actual physical size of the two-dimensional statement to the human figure. Contemporary paintings of monumental physical dimensions are examples of this method. For instance, without considering any other aspects of the work, James Rosenquist's $102 \times 223\frac{1}{2}$-in. painting (Figure 2) cannot help but have an effect on the viewer simply because of its size.

Another way we can create contrast of scale in a two-dimensional work is by comparing an image to the area it occupies in a given frame of reference. For instance, if an object occupies a large part of its frame of reference, it may appear massive in relation to the small amount of unoccupied space. Figure 3 demonstrates how the comparison of occupied and unoc-

3

Catalogue cover by George Canciani for WBZ-TV, Boston

2

James Rosenquist, *Paper Clip,* 1973, 8′ 6″ x 18′ 7½″. Dallas Museum of Fine Arts

cupied space can be used to make a baseball seem monumental in size. By reversing the emphasis, Jim Dine evokes a different type of drama in his painting (Figure 4). The toothbrushes appear small in comparison to the surrounding unoccupied area.

A third way in which we can achieve two-dimensional contrast of scale within a single frame of reference is by direct comparison of dimensionally recognizable objects. This type of scale relationship can be seen in an illustration by Brad Holland (Figure 5) and a painting by Magritte (Figure 6). These examples emphasize the fact that this kind of scale contrast depends on the use of dimensionally recognizable imagery.

5

Editorial cartoon by Brad Holland, © by The New York Times Company. Reprinted by permission

4

6

Rene Magritte, *The Listening Chamber*, 1953. © by ADAGP, Paris 1981

Jim Dine, *A Bathroom Study*, 1962. Courtesy of The Pace Gallery

Two- and three-dimensional contrast of scale can be accomplished by directly comparing two or more objects of either unknown or undetermined dimension. An example of this can be seen in Figure 7. This diagram contains three squares; visually, one is large and two are small. These squares could represent any size, since nonrepresentational images have no predetermined dimension. In this example, the large square is really not large in relation to the picture plane, but it seems so when compared to the two smaller ones.

Differences in size between nonrepresentational components are frequently used in typography to create visual contrast. For example, in Figure 8 the dramatic impact created is the direct result of a scale comparison between the large letter form and the size of the box. This method of contrast of scale is also used by nonob-jective abstract artists, craftspeople, and architects. In the painting by Scott Reagan (Figure 9), visual interest is achieved by effectively contrasting the scale of two rectilinear shapes and one curvilinear shape. This type of contrast was effectively used in the design of a site model for the Kimbell Museum of Art (Figure 10). When viewed from above, it is apparent that the architect, Louis Kahn, joined two massive roofed areas with a third smaller one. This dramatic contrast might have been felt inside the building even though it could not have been seen from above.

7

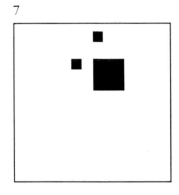

8

Package designed by Milton Glaser/Seymour Chwast for Higgins, Inc., Courtesy Faber-Castell Corporation

9. Scott Reagan, *Untitled*

Site Model, Kimbell Art Museum ("H" plan), constructed, November 1967. Architect, Louis Kahn

Establishing a visual comparison among a number of objects—few objects to many—is still another method for achieving contrast of scale. For example, even though the rectilinear shapes in Figure 11 are similar in size, a contrast of scale is accomplished by the comparison of a small number of shapes to a large number. A three-dimensional example of this method of contrast can be seen in the theater designed by Mies Van Der Rohe (Figure 12). Contrast of scale is acieved by comparing visually the number of vertical columns. Seven large vertical columns create the structural framework of the building, which contrasts with the remaining number of smaller vertical columns that make up the façade of the theater.

13

tonhalle, grosser saal
donnerstag, 10. märz
20.15 uhr, 1960
16. volkskonzert der
tonhalle-gesellschaft
zürich
leitung
erich schmid
solisten
annie laffra
violoncello
eva maria rogner
sopran

musica viva

hans werner henze
sonata per archi
luigi dallapiccola
‹concerto per la notte
di natale dall'anno
1956› für sopran und
kammerorchester
arthur honegger
konzert für violoncello
und orchester
henri dutilleux
erste sinfonie
karten zu fr. 1.-, 2.-, 3.-
tonhalle, hug, jecklin
kuoni, dep. kasse oer-
likon, kreditanstalt

Poster designed by J. Müller-Brockmann
for Tonhalle-Gesellschaft, Zurich SWI

11

12

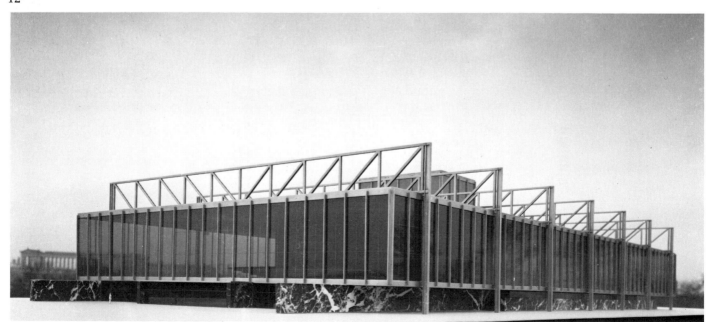

Project for National Theatre, Mannheim, Germany by Mies Van Der Rohe, Photograph Hedrich-Blessing

Figure 13, a poster design, is a two-dimensional typographic example based on scale contrast achieved by comparing numbers of objects. In this poster, an impressive scale contrast is achieved by comparing few to many—the two words on the left to the large number of words on the right.

## CONTRAST OF SHAPE/VOLUME

Contrast of shape can be achieved by comparing the visual characteristics of a shape to those of any other shape—circle to square, triangle to rectangle. Contrast of volume can be accomplished by comparing volume to volume—cone to cylinder, cube to sphere. And finally, contrast of shape/volume can be created by comparing shape to volume—circle to sphere, square to cylinder.

A specific example of the use of contrast of volume can be seen in the Gabriel Kahn sculpture in Figure 14. In this work, Kahn creates a dramatic contrast of curvilinear volumes to rectilinear ones. Another strong contrast—organic volumes to geometric ones—can be seen in the Arp sculpture in Figure 15. In the painting *Seven*

14

15

Jean Arp, *Star,* 1939–60.
Collection Edouard Loeb, Paris

Gabriel Kahn, *Nantucket,* 1960. Hirshhorn Museum & Sculpture Garden, Smithsonian Institution

*Jellied Apples* by Wayne Thiebaud (Figure 16), the use of contrast brings otherwise ordinary subject matter to life. The apples have been painted to appear volumetric in relation to the flat, rectangular shape of the picture plane. Visual drama is created in the house designed by Frank Lloyd Wright shown in Figure 18 as a result of juxtaposing the geometric volumes of the house with the organic forms of the surrounding environment. In the painting by Joan Miró (Figure 17), visual activity is accomplished by the use of a number of contrasts of shape—triangles to squares, geometric circles to organic ovals, rectilinear shapes to curvilinear, simple to complex.

All these examples demonstrate how versatile the use of contrast of shape/volume can be. As with any other visual tool, it can be used in an isolated instance or in any number of combinations with other contrasts and/or visual methods.

16

Wayne Thiebaud, *Seven Jellied Apples,* Collection Allan Stone Gallery

17. Joan Miro, *The Poetess,* 1940. Collection Mr. and Mrs. Ralph F. Colin, New York

Kaufman House, Fallingwater, Bear Run, Pennsylvania, 1936 by Frank Lloyd Wright. Photograph Hedrich-Blessing

## CONTRAST OF DIRECTION

In Chapter 1, we established that certain shapes and volumes can appear to travel in specific directions. By contrasting the direction of shapes and volumes, versatile visual statements can be achieved. For instance, contrast of direction can be used to suggest visual opposition (Figure 19), visual activity (Figure 20), or visual tension (Figure 21).

Robert Cremean, *Swinging Woman,*
Collection University of Nebraska, Sheldon Memorial Art Gallery
Wood mache, 1960. 58 x 35 x 1/2 x 67 in.

22

19

20

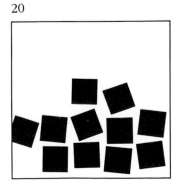

21

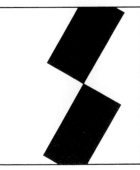

In the sculpture titled *Swinging Woman* (Figure 22), a contrast of direction between the two major volumes—the woman and the support—is used to communicate the motion. In a similar way, Pierre Bonnard created a feeling of directional motion in his painting *Self Portrait* (Figure 23). In this work, most of the shapes assume one of three directional attitudes—horizontal, vertical, or diagonal. The overall visual result is dramatic and dynamic, even though the individual components are static and passive.

23

Pierre Bonnard, *Self-Portrait in Dressing-Room Mirror,* 1940, oil on canvas, 76.2 x 61 cm. Bought 1971, Art Gallery of New South Wales, Sydney

## CONTRAST OF VALUE

*Color* can be defined as the property of reflecting light waves of a particular length. A combination of varying proportions of white (reflecting all light waves) and black (absorbing all light waves) results in neutral gray. Although colors and neutral grays are essentially different, they share a common characteristic—value.

*Value* is the tonal quality—light or dark—of a color or neutral gray. Every color and neutral gray can be varied from very light to very dark to achieve a full range of value. The most extreme contrast of value possible is white to black. White is the lightest possible value; black is the darkest. A comparative relationship between these two extremes creates maximum value contrast. An example can be seen in the comparative relationship established between figure and ground in Figure 24. The selection of any other two values would not appear as bold or as strong. For this reason, maximum value contrast is frequently used when visual strength is essential, as in books, magazines, and newspapers. Most of these are printed black on white to make the typography more legible. This helps to reinforce the primary intent—the communication of information.

Black to white is the maximum value contrast, but there are an infinite number of other value contrasts. Figure 25 presents five figure-ground relationships of value contrast. In the first, diagram A, the value contrast between figure and ground is very slight. In diagrams B, C, D, and E, the figure-ground contrast becomes progressively greater, with the most extreme contrast—and the least integration—occurring in diagram E. This demonstrates the fact that the greater the contrast in value between figure and ground, the more dramatic the visual impact of the image can be. It also indicates that the greater the value contrast between figure and ground, the stronger the visual separation can be.

When trying to maintain visual impact and still avoid visual separation, the artist may find it necessary to use some form of transition with maximum value contrast. Transition lessens the disparity between black and white. The basic way to accomplish this is to introduce varying values of gray into a black and white composition. It is then possible to obtain dramatic—as well as cohesive—results.

Finally, we can apply value contrast in a visual gestalt to alter or control composition. Examples can be seen in Figure 26, which presents a progressive series of compositions consisting of twelve squares on a ground. The first composition is limited to two values of gray; the results are neither dramatic nor lively. The second composition is limited to three values; the visual effect is more interesting than that created by the first composition, but it is not appreciably more dramatic or lively. As fewer value limitations are imposed on each of these progressive compositions, the visual effect becomes more vital and dramatic. Although the arrangement of the twelve squares remains constant throughout the examples, a variety of compositional gestalts has been achieved simply by adjusting the contrast in value of the squares.

24

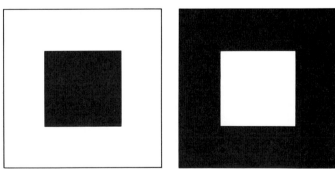

25

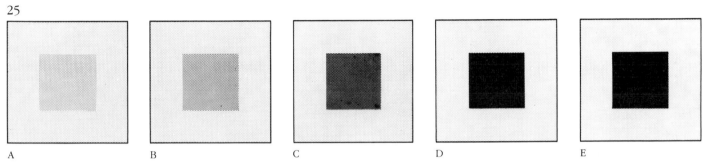

A         B         C         D         E

26

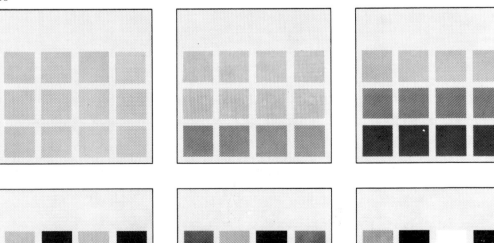

Once the visual potentials of contrast of value have been explored, they can be applied in a number of combinations. One excellent example of an artist's making use of maximum value contrast can be seen in George Segal's *The Execution* (Figure 27). The explicit content communicated by the title and imagery of this sculpture is effectively reinforced by the stark value contrast between the white plaster figures and the dark background. This shows how strong contrast of value can create a harshness or starkness when it is desired. There is little doubt that any of these figures is dead, and the hanging figure unquestionably communicates brutality and violence.

Unlike Segal's stark sculpture, Vermeer's *A Woman Weighing Gold* (Figure 28) combines rich tonality of value contrast for dramatic impact. Maxim value contrast has been used to dramatize the woman, but the dark surroundings appear comfortable rather than harsh, and the woman seems to be a natural part of the rich environment.

27

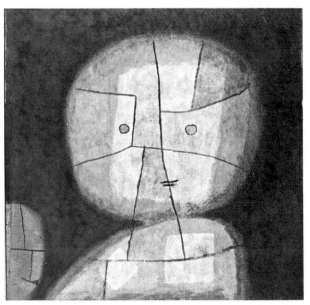

To achieve an equally dramatic visual effect, Paul Klee's *Bust of a Child* (Figure 29) uses a more subtle value contrast than Vermeer's painting. Multiple close values are used to create a soft, rich tonality within the childlike figure. The artist subtly contrasts this figure with the dark background by establishing transitions between the two with a network of dark lines and a graduation of light to dark from the center of the figure outward. An overall impression of soft richness has been effectively combined with dramatic visual impact to communicate the artist's emotional and intellectual intent.

29. Paul Klee, *Bust of a Child,* 1933.
(c)1981, Copyright by COSMOPRESS, Geneva & ADAGP, Paris

28

Jan Vermeer, *Woman Holding A Balance*. National Gallery of Art, Washington. Widener Collection

## CONTRAST OF SURFACE

All objects have surface qualities that can range from very smooth to very rough. These characteristics are often referred to as texture. Usually, texture appeals to our sense of touch. However, when something can only be seen and not felt, it is possible—from prior experience and knowledge—for us to re-create the sensory perception of touch. This recalled perception can be visually activated by the light and dark value patterns usually associated with various surface textures. For instance, if we touch a highly polished surface, the sensation of "smooth" is mentally recorded and can be recalled when seeing such a surface again. In the same way, when surfaces with a marked degree of patterned value contrast are seen, they are expected to be rough to the touch. As a result of our prior sensory experience and knowledge, it is possible for us to create and communicate the illusion of texture.

Just as certain surface qualities can be associated with tactile sensations, so they can also create certain emotional feelings. For instance, surfaces of woven textures can feel emotionally warm, accessible, or human. In comparison, many smooth, polished surfaces can appear cooly intellectual, unapproachable, mechanical, or austere. By contrast of surface, all these tactile and emotional characteristics can be varied and combined effectively to enrich both two- and three-dimensional expressions.

For example, Jane Cheatham's painting (Figure 30) exhibits a number of contrasting, illusory surfaces—from the highly textured patterns of ropelike fringe to the smoothness of draped fabric, and from the reflective smoothness of lustrous pearls to the dull sheen of hard, worn bone. All these contrasts of surface interact to create visual depth and richness.

30

Jane Hart Cheatham, *Passages,* 1977. Private collection

31. Taj Mahal, Agra, India. Photograph courtesy Elizabeth Skidmore Sasser

Lincoln Center (Left: Metropolitan Opera House; Right: Vivian Beaumont Theater), 1965 by Eero Saarinen, Photograph Bob Serating

## CONTRAST AS ACCENT

Architects also make use of contrasting surfaces to dramatize their expressions. They utilize not only the surface characteristics of various building materials—brick, steel, glass, wood—but also the surface characteristics created by the natural environment—trees, plants, water. Two examples of the way these various surfaces can be dramatically contrasted are shown in the architectural expressions of Figure 31 and Figure 32.

When a single proportionately small characteristic contrasts with the overall visual expression, it is often referred to as an *accent.* We can effectively use accents to draw attention to a particular area of a composition. The use of accents can be seen in *Sam Who Walked Alone By Night* by David Hockney (Figure 33). The very dark areas behind the head, in the eye, on the chest, and across the trunk focus the attention on the figure and give the work a feeling of vitality.

Accents can also be used to direct and pace a viewer's attention throughout an entire expression. As a result of thoughtful placement, accents move the eye from place to place. Paul Klee's *Family Walk* (Figure 34) uses dark accents to pace and direct attention horizontally across the entire drawing.

33

34

Paul Klee, *Family Walk,* 1930. (c)1981, Copyright by COSMOPRESS, Geneva & ADAGP, Paris

David Hockney, *Sam Who Walked Alone By Night,* oil on canvas, 36″ x 24″.
(c)David Hockney 1961, Courtesy Petersburg Press

# SECTION ONE

# 6

LINE

Primitive people first used line to indicate symbols; babies use line in their first scribbling ventures; young children use line when learning to draw letters of the alphabet, and so on. Line is the most primary, the most direct, and the oldest method of creating visual expressions.

Generally, line may be thought of as a thin, thread-like mark. However, for the specific purposes of design, we can consider the visual and communicative ramifications of line beyond primary marking. An infinite variety of lines can be created. They may be blurred, scratched, dotted, thick, thin, light, dark; they may be made with pencil, pen, brush, sticks, strings—almost anything.

Since it is possible for us to create an endless variety of lines in innumerable ways, it would not be practical to consider each kind individually. Therefore, for general discussion and understanding, we can classify line into four basic categories.

## CLASSIFICATIONS OF LINE

The first category of line is *even-weight*. This type of line is characterized by a consistency of thickness, or value, throughout its length. Even-weight line may appear to be sharp, precise, and mechanical, as in Figure 1. Or, it may appear more spontaneous and delicate, as in Figure 2. Even-weight line can be spontaneous and heavy without being precisely controlled, as in Figure 3. In addition to these characteristics, we can think of even-weight line as having a stable quality that defines the edges of shapes. Finally, even-weight line may be seen as being very economical and, by itself, may do little to provoke an emotional response.

1

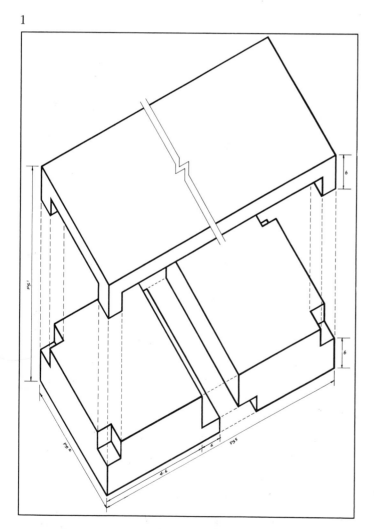

2

Etruscan Amphora, 600 B.C. Dallas Museum of Fine Arts gift of Mr. and Mrs. Cecil H. Green

3

Henri Matisse, *The Red Room,* 1947. (c) S.P.A.D.E.M., Paris/V.A.G.A., New York, 1981

A second classification of line that we can establish is *thick-to-thin*. This type of line varies in weight throughout its length and can appear to have value variation. Figure 4 illustrates how thick-to-thin line can help enhance the illusion of form. The roundness of the cylinder on the left is more apparent than the one on the right because of the heavier line weight at the rounded corners. Thick-to-thin line also can give visual variety to

a completed expression without necessarily creating the illusion of space or form as Figure 5 shows.

*Light-to-dark* is another general category of line and can function in much the same way as thick-to-thin. The major difference between the two is that variety is achieved through value variation rather than weight variation. This is possible since light-to-dark line, unlike thick-to-thin, has even weight throughout its length. Like thick-to-thin line, light-to-dark can also enhance the illusion of depth and volume (Figure 6). An example can be seen in the Jean-Auguste Dominique Ingres drawing in Figure 7. Light-to-dark line has been utilized effec-

4

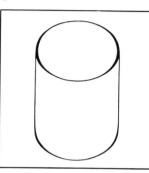 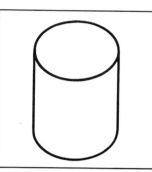

5

*Profile of one of the Ramesses, portrayed as Osiris,*
sketch from a tomb painting, 20th Dynasty. The Louvre, Paris

tively in delineating the forward leg to reinforce its position and depth. To dramatize the fullness and projection of the form, the dark portion of the line has been placed where the form curves and changes direction. When illusion is not necessarily the objective, light-to-dark line can create variety in visual pacing, as in Paul Klee's drawing *Baptismal Font* (Figure 8).

7

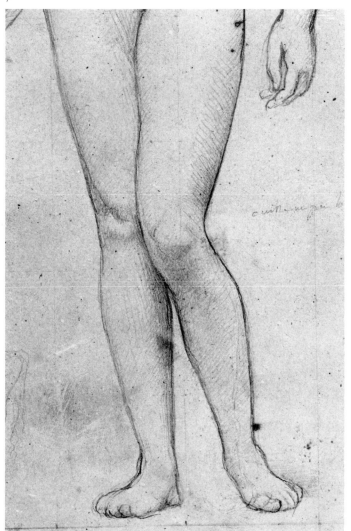

Jean Auguste Ingres, *Studies of a Man and Woman for 'The Golden Age,'* 1842, detail. Courtesy of the Fogg Art Museum Harvard University, Bequest-Greenville L. Winthrop

6

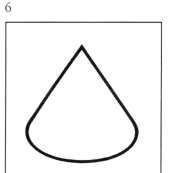 

8

Paul Klee, *Baptismal Font.*
©1981, Copyright by COSMOPRESS, Geneva & ADAGP, Paris,

The final category of line, *broken,* is self-explanatory; throughout its length it appears to be interrupted. A broken line may vary in weight or value, and on occasion may give the impression of being erratic or nervous (Figure 9). It can also be found in works illustrating mechanical precision (Figure 10). The broken line category is frequently associated with sketches because of its direct, spontaneous quality (Figure 11). Finally, broken line can have a very direct, graphic quality that is neither sketchy nor mechanical. An example of this can be seen in Klee's drawing *Child and Phantom* (Figure 12).

9

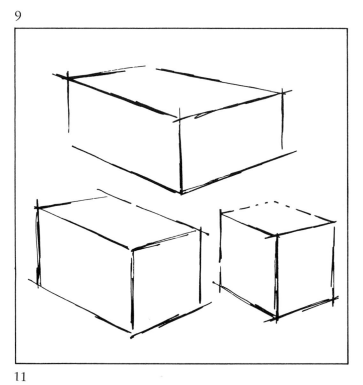

10

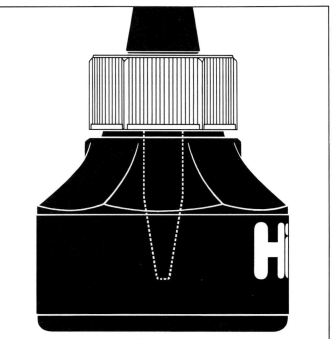

11

12

Paul Klee, *Child and Phantom,* 1938.

## LINE USAGE

The expressive potential of each of these four categories of line is endless. As a result, the type of line, or the combination of types, we use will depend directly on and relate to the idea we wish to express. For instance, in Edgar Degas' drawing *Dancer Adjusting Her Slipper* (Figure 13), a combination of all four types has been used with an emphasis on two of them, thick-to-thin and light-to-dark. Degas has effectively used line in this drawing to express the lyrical quality of the ballet, as well as to suggest the illusion of form.

13

Edgar Degas, *Dancer Adjusting Slipper,* 1873. The Metropolitan Museum of Art, Bequest of Mrs. H.O. Havemeyer, 1929. The H.O. Havemeyer Collection

It is difficult for us to imagine the same form and idea of the Degas drawing being expressed as convincingly with even-weight, heavy lines. However, in a different situation these lines could be just as expressive. For example, even-weight, heavy lines are not only appropriate but very effective in conveying the imagery and content of Paul Klee's *They All Run After* (Figure 14).

Line often assumes a secondary role in visual expressions. For instance, in Mary Cassat's drawing *The Banjo Player* (Figure 15), thick-to-thin line directs the eye to the nonlinear focal points of the upper clothing and heads. In some situations, line loses its linear characteristic and performs as value instead. In the study of a boy's face (Figure 16), for example, even-weight and light-to-dark lines have been placed

close together to create a larger pattern of value that conveys form instead of line. Such treatments of line can be used to give the same visual strength that value or color possesses.

Although line is usually thought of in relation to drawing and the graphic arts, it can also be used convincingly in painting. Andrew Wyeth's haunting *Wind from the Sea* (Figure 17) exhibits even-weight, delicate line in the imagery of the billowing lace curtains. *Veteran in a New Field* by Winslow Homer (Figure 18) contains combinations of broken and thick-to-thin line that appear as grass rather than line.

14

Paul Klee, *They All Run After,* 1940.
(c) 1981, Copyright by COSMOPRESS,
Geneva & ADAGP, Paris

16. Jane Hart Cheatham, sketch 1971

15

Mary Cassatt, *The Banjo Lesson.*
Prints and Photographs Division, Library of Congress, Pennell Collection

17

Andrew Wyeth, *Wind From The Sea,* 1947. Private Collection

18

Winslow Homer, *The Veteran in a New Field.* The Metropolitan Museum of Art,
Bequest of Miss Adelaide Milton De Groot (1876–1967), 1967

*19*

The side of the mask in Figure 19 illustrates the use of decorative incising to create linear elements. In addition, thick-to-thin linear forms that cause contrast of direction as well as texture can be seen in the raffia surrounding the mask's face and shoulders.

Finally, line in its most familiar form occurs as a combination of all basic types; this is the calligraphic form known as handwriting (Figure 20). Alan E. Cober has used his own handwriting to create a sense of spontaneity and immediacy in his illustration concerning prescriptions for the aged (Figure 22). A more formal visual expression of handwriting can be seen in many typefaces. For example, elegant Formal Script type is based on the thick-to-thin qualities of handwriting and can elicit an emotional response. In the design of a photographer's business card (Figure 21), formal script was used to communicate the emotional content of one of his specialties—weddings.

20

Mask, *Kifwebe,* Songe, Africa; Zaire. Dallas Museum of Fine Arts, the Gustave and Franyo Schindler Collection of African Sculpture, Gift of the McDermott Foundation in Honor of Eugene McDermott

Pablo Picasso brush drawn painting signature

21

*Robert Suddarth*
*Photographer*
*Phone (806) 795-4553*
*3402 73rd Suite d*
*Lubbock, Texas 79423*

Business card designed by Frank Cheatham

22

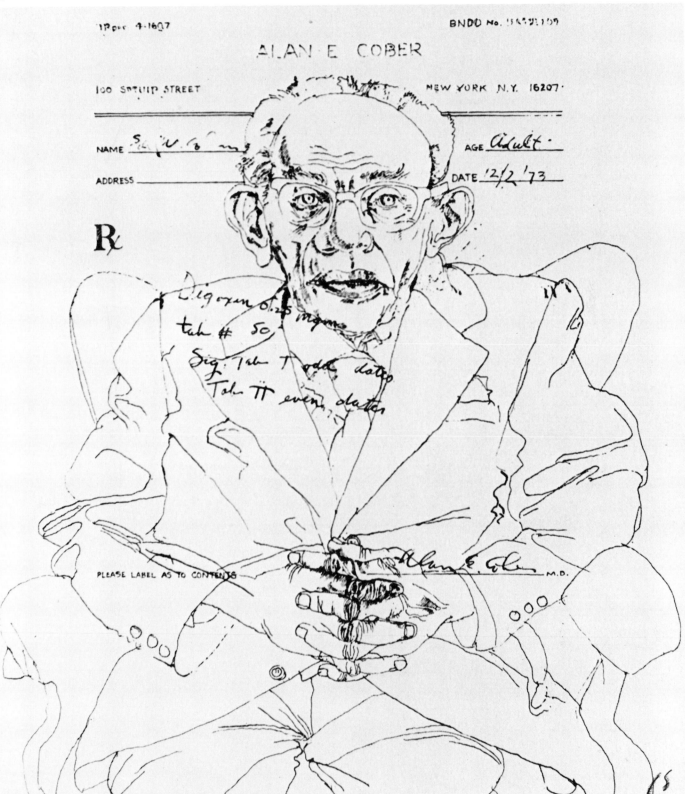

Illustration by Alan E. Cober for *Emergency Medicine*

# SECTION ONE

# 7

**REPETITION**

In design, repetition occurs when any individual component is used more than once. Because we can use repetition so simply and successfully to create unified visual statements, it is probably one of the oldest elements of design.

The quality of reinforcement is one reason for the success of repetition. Whenever a component is repeated, it functions like a beat in a rhythm; each beat reinforces its predecessor by duplication. Psychologically, we easily respond to this reinforced duplication because both our bodies and our lives, in one form or another, are a series of repetitive events. The human heart beats in a repetitive manner to pump a continuous flow of blood throughout the body. The structure of the human spine is a series of repetitive forms known as vertebrae. We eat, sleep, and breathe repetitively. Most of what we see is repetitive: leaves on trees, houses on streets, fingers on hands, toes on feet.

While repetition has the potential to create visual continuity and strength, it can also be monotonous and boring if not alleviated. The dull, droning sound of a speaker's voice repeating one tone over and over can become very monotonous. Unaltered repetition in any individual's activities can result in boring patterns. Similarly, visual repetition that is unvaried can produce dull and boring results (Figure 1). To avoid this, deviation from the regular arrangement—anomaly—can be introduced into a composition to create needed visual variety (Figure 2).

## TYPES OF REPETITION

We can combine and recombine elements of repetition in an infinite number of applications and forms to obtain a variety of results. However, for purposes of analysis we can simplify these elements into four basic categories: shape/volume, size, position, and direction.

### Repetition of Shape/Volume

This type of repetition occurs when a shape or volume is repeated within a single work. With this type, the shape or form maintains the same configuration throughout to give the gestalt a strong cohesiveness. Paul Klee's *Portal of a Mosque* (Figure 3) is an excellent example of repetition of shape. The small individual rectangles in the work are proportionately repetitive of the overall rectangle of the picture plane as well as of each other. To avoid a static quality, anomaly of value and color has been introduced throughout the composition.

Repetition of volume is also apparent in Sheryl Haler's sculptural work (Figure 4). The primary volume used to unify this piece is a cylinder. For variation the diameters differ and some are flattened; but the cylindrical configuration has been kept constant. Circular forms have also been repeated, varied only in size. The inclusion of yarns shaped into organic forms avoids the tedium that could occur with so much repetition of volume.

1         2

4

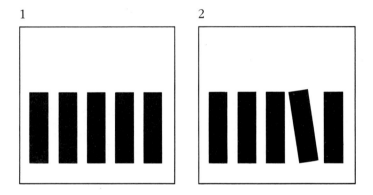

Sheryl Haler, *Untitled,* 1979

3

Paul Klee, *Portal of a Mosque,* 1931. Collection Mr. and Mrs. Ralph F. Colin, New York

## Repetition of Size

In this type of repetition, part or all of the shapes or forms in a work are of the same size. The shapes or forms may change in configuration, but visual unity is maintained by constancy of size (Figure 5).

*California Series No. 3* by Jane Cheatham (Figure 6) is an example of repetition of size. The figures on either side of the painting are identical in size and appear to enclose the deep space portion in the center. In addition, the linear shapes in the center are essentially the same width. The repetition occuring in these areas provides structure and unity in this work.

5

6

Jane Hart Cheatham, *California Series, No. 3*, 1980. Private Collection

Repetition of size and form is also demonstrated in Jasper John's *Target with Four Faces* (Figure 7). The four faces aligned at the top of the work are not only the same size physically, they are also repetitive in configuration. Similarly, the three rectangular forms separating the faces are the same repeated size and shape. Finally, the contrast between the organic forms of the faces and the geometric rectangles separating them creates repetition with variation that helps to make this work visually strong and dynamic.

7

Jasper Johns, *Target with Four Faces,* 1955, Encaustic on newspaper over canvas, 26 x 26″ surmounted by four tinted plaster faces in wood box with hinged front. Box closed, 3 3/4 x 26 x 3 1/2″. Overall dimensions with box open, 33 5/8 x 26 x 3″. Collection, The Museum of Modern Art, New York. Gift of Mr. and Ms. Robert C. Scull

## Repetition of Position

Repetition of position can be used as an organizational method to unify similar or dissimilar shapes and forms. Basically, repetition of position occurs when visual elements are placed along a common physical or optical alignment (Figures 8 and 9).

Repetition of position unifies the magazine cover designed by Seymour Chwast (Figure 10). All the pens have been effectively organized by positioning them so that all the tops are lined up on a common horizontal optical alignment. Additionally, they are all placed visually equidistant from one another. The strong repetitive quality is offset by asymmetrically positioning the entire group of pens low on the page.

8

9

11

Pre-Columbian, Yucatan, Chichén Itźa, Photograph courtesy Division of Architecture, Texas Tech University

Repetition of position unifies Figure 11 both horizontally and vertically. The long horizontal physical alignments repeated on the entire face of the building physically and visually support and unify the vertical elements. Also adding to the visual strength of the façade is the repeated positioning of the vertical sculptural forms between the horizontal divisions; that is, the vertical forms in the lowest frieze are the same distance from one another as are those in each successive frieze. Finally, anomaly is effectively created by the slightly irregular shape of each rough hewn stone.

10

Magazine cover designed by Seymour Chwast for *Idea*. Courtesy Seibundo Shinkosha Publishing Co., LTD

## Repetition of Direction

The configuration of certain shapes and forms imply direction; others do not (Figure 12). When directional shapes and forms are repeated, repetition of direction occurs. Such repetition reinforces visual directional movement (Figure 13).

The use of varying amounts of both repetition of direction and change of direction have produced powerful optical stimulation in Victor Vasarely's *Tau-Ceti* (Figure 14). Careful analysis of this work reveals that the top two rows of repetitive squares imply no apparent direction. The third row repeats parallelograms visually moving to the left until a single parallelogram suddenly changes direction to the right. This type of mo-

12

13

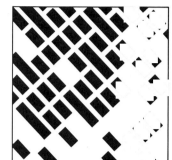

14. Victor Vasarely, *Tau-Ceti,* 1955–65. Collection of the artist

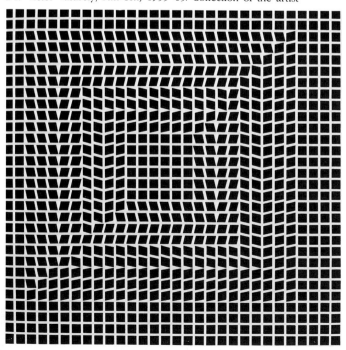

tion and countermotion is repeated with careful variation throughout most of the composition.

Repetition of direction is exemplified in *Rock-Rock* by Richard Lindner (Figure 15). A vigorous vertical movement is created by repeating certain shapes in the center—the vertical strings, the shape on which they exist, and the vertical stripes on the collar. This action is reinforced by the vertical direction of the picture plane. A horizontal counterthrust is achieved through the use of repeated stripes on the arms. Anomaly can be seen in the background since each of those shapes travels in a different direction to a common center.

15. Richard Lindner, *Rock-Rock*, 1966–67. Dallas Museum of Fine Arts, Gift of Mr. and Mrs. James H. Clark

# SECTION ONE

# 8

TIME, CHANGE, AND MOTION

## PERCEPTION OF VISUAL SEQUENCES

Sometimes we, as artists, are confronted with the need to communicate visually any of three conditions: a passage of time, a change in appearance, or an object in motion. Time, change, and motion all incorporate characteristics of each other. For instance, a passage of time involves a physical change in appearance; while time passes, the visual configuration of a clock's face also changes by a continuous left-to-right rotational motion of the clock's hands. Therefore, to be concerned with one of these conditions is to be concerned with all of them.

In stationary forms, time, change, and motion possess characteristics that enable them to be communicated visually through the use of *sequence*—a visual property that utilizes a particular order of succession, or following. A visual sequence can be defined as a series of related stationary images used one after another in a particular order to communicate the passage of time, the occurrence of change, or the action of motion. Basically we can use two methods to stage visual sequences. One utilizes multiple stationary frames of reference; the other employs a single stationary frame. In all other respects, these two methods are the same and can be used in either two- or three-dimensional visual expressions.

Ordinary comic strips are classic examples of visual sequences presented in multiple stationary frames of reference. This particular method is achieved visually by dividing the message into a number of individual segments which are then presented in an ordered, progressive sequence. Such a presentation is comprehensible because we have been conditioned to read verbal sequences in the same way. For example, the text on this page is a verbal sequence that begins in the upper left corner, moves progressively from left to right, then drops down to the next line and begins again at the left. This process is repeated until all the desired information has been communicated. As a result of this verbal conditioning, we can read images presented in this same order. Figure 1 shows two examples of progressive number sequences in multiple stationary frames of reference that we can read like verbal messages.

These examples are characteristic of the use of sequences in verbal communication, but there are many variations on verbal sequences. For instance, in Figure 2, example C is the direct counterpart of example B in Figure 1; it has just been organized in a single frame of reference. In the next example, D, the variation from A of Figure 1 simply lies in the order of presentation—there is no left-to-right order. But the verbal sequence characteristic of reading from top to bottom remains, so we are still able to interpret the example. In example E, we can read the order of the sequence progression in either of two ways—from the inside to the outside or the outside to the inside—depending on the visual emphasis.

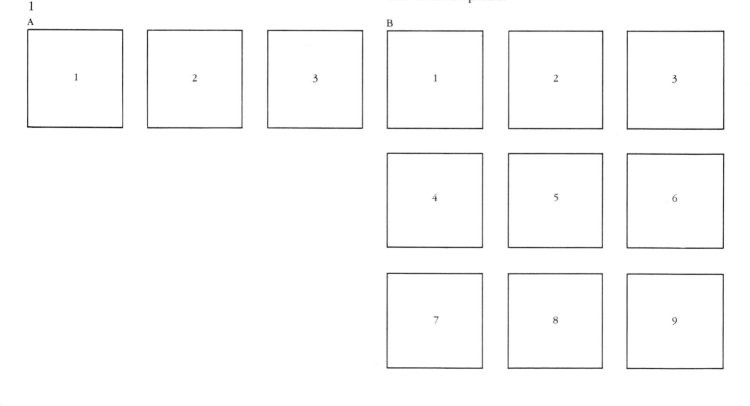

1

A

| 1 | 2 | 3 |

B

| 1 | 2 | 3 |
| 4 | 5 | 6 |
| 7 | 8 | 9 |

When using visual sequences in both multiple and single frames of reference, an important factor to be considered is the number of frames needed to communicate successfully. Usually, sequences that incorporate at least five frames in a multiple situation, or those that use at least five progressive images in a single frame of reference, seem to communicate to us in a smoother, more comprehensible manner than sequences with fewer visual stages. In certain situations it may be possible to communicate with less than five, but usually clear communication is facilitated by at least five steps or more. The more sequence steps used, the slower the transition from one phase to the next and the more dramatic the visual difference can be from the first to the last frame. However, a great number of steps can also become visually redundant and require too much space to function, so a balance between too few and too many steps must be reached.

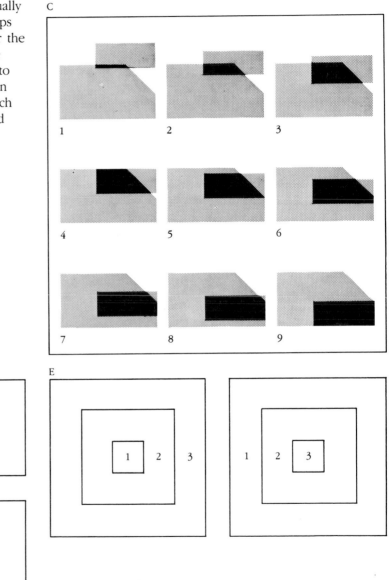

## SEQUENCES IN STATIONARY FRAMES OF REFERENCE

There are several basic sequences we can use in stationary frames of reference:

1. Additive sequence

2. Subtractive sequence

3. Direction-change sequence

4. Size-change sequence

5. Position-change sequence

6. Metamorphic sequence

7. Distortion/destruction sequence

Any of these seven can be used to communicate the passage of time, change in appearance, or the action of motion. Depending on the desired communication and the physical limitations imposed by the problem, one type of sequence—or a combination of several types—may prove to be more effective than others. A functional selection of a sequence or sequences requires nothing more than familiarity with the possible methods and a clear idea of what is to be communicated. Then it is merely a matter of making visual application.

3

4

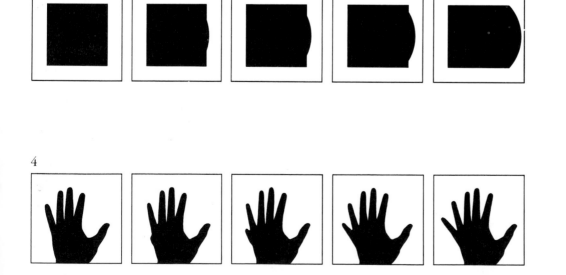

## Additive Sequence

An additive sequence is composed of two- or three-dimensional images that progressively develop additional visual characteristics.

Figures 3 and 4 present examples of additive sequences. Figure 3 shows a square as it develops a curved convex side in a progressive sequence from left to right; and Figure 4 demonstrates an additive sequence using a hand that progressively develops an additional finger.

In Figure 5, the designer Milton Glaser uses an additive sequence in a poster design to advertise a French literary magazine. This example is identical to the sequences presented in Figures 3 and 4; in contrast,

Figure 6 utilizes a different type of additive sequence. In this case, the numbers of silhouetted figures in each progressive frame of the sequence are increased rather than one image being altered by addition.

All four of these examples are additive sequences that progressively develop visual characteristics to communicate a physical change in appearance.

5

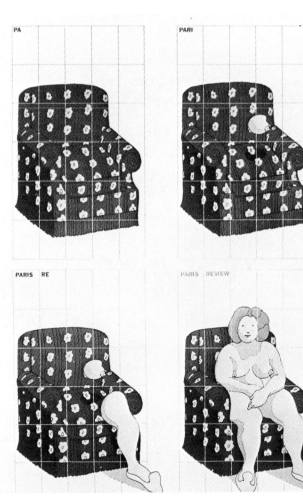

Silkscreen poster designed by Milton Glaser,
Courtesy *The Paris Review*

6

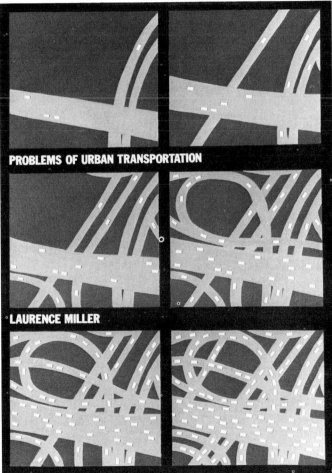

Student bookcover design, Keith Owens

## Subtractive Sequence

A subtractive sequence—the exact opposite of an additive one—is composed of two- or three-dimensional imagery that progressively deletes portions of the original image.

The first two examples given for additive sequence (Figures 3 and 4) have been repositioned in reverse order from left to right to create two subtractive sequences (Figure 7). Figure 8 is an example of a subtractive sequence in multiple frames of reference. On this booklet cover, the image of a man seems to be sinking into the floor because portions of his image are being deleted.

We can effectively combine additive and subtractive sequences to communicate the appearance and disappearance of images. Seymour Chwast uses a combination of these two types in an amusing poster designed for a retrospective exhibition on the subject of design, illustration, and photography (Figure 9).

8

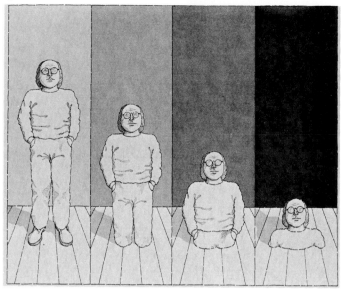

Design by David Ashton, Illustration by David Franek for Sinai Hospital Auxiliary Inc., Baltimore

7

Announcement of a retrospective design exhibition
designed by Seymour Chwast, Courtesy The Meade Library of Ideas

### Direction—Change Sequence

A direction-change sequence is a visual sequence used to communicate a change in the way a two- or three-dimensional element faces, points, or moves in space.

An example of a direction-change sequence can be seen in Figure 10. From left to right in relation to the picture plane, the horizontal and vertical positioning of the pictured square changes to assume a diagonal position. This direction change is implemented by sequentially rotating the square clockwise so that it appears to have moved.

Thomas Eakins' photograph of a man pole-vaulting (Figure 11) illustrates a direction change sequence that creates the illusion of motion. In this example, movement occurs visually by showing the various configurations the human body assumes as it moves through space.

10

11

Thomas Eakins, *Pole-Vaulter: Multiple Exposure Photograph of George Reynolds,* 1884.
The Metropolitan Museum of Art, Gift of George Bregler

## Size—Change Sequence

A size-change sequence is used to communicate, either two- or three-dimensionally, a visual change in size—small to large or large to small.

Figure 12 shows, from left to right, how a very small circular dot can become a large one through a progressive series of visual steps. This example specifically employs the image of a two-dimensional circle, but any two- or three-dimensional image could be visually or physically increased in size this way. Figure 13 presents a size-change sequence that uses the three-dimensional image of a man. As this sequence is viewed from left to right, the man appears to grow progressively smaller just as the circle grew larger in the previous example.

12

13

Photographer: Maggy Cuesta

Like the other types of sequences that have been discussed, size-change sequences can function in multiple frames of reference—as in Figures 12 and 13—or in single frames of reference. Figures 14 and 15 are examples of size-change sequences that occur in a single frame of reference. In Figure 14, two-dimensional imagery that sequentially changes in size can be seen in a poster designed to announce an art show concerned with landscapes. Figure 15 uses three-dimensional imagery to create the same effect for a poster promoting a British real estate development.

## Position—Change Sequence

A position-change sequence progressively varies the placement of two- or three-dimensional components to communicate motion.

In Figure 16, a large circle appears to move progressively to the right until it vanishes from the frame of reference. A feeling of motion is created as a result of the position changes of the circle in each progressive frame. Similarly, Figure 17 presents movement, but of two images rather than just one. In this example, one image moves out of the picture plane while another moves into it. In these particular sequences, the motion is slow; but this is not always the case. For instance, the *Pirelli Presenter* (Figure 18) creates a feeling of rapid motion by using a series of abrupt position changes to communicate a figure balancing on a circular shape.

15

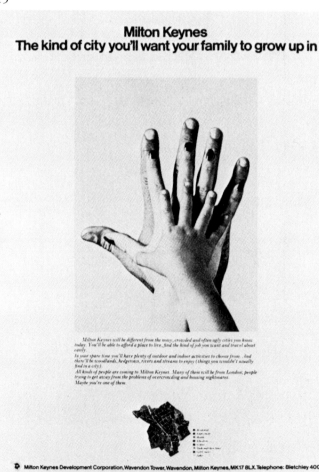

Poster designed by Harry Scotting/M. Minale/B. Tatterfield/A. Maranzano for Milton Keynes City, GBR.
Courtesy Milton Keynes Development Corporation

14

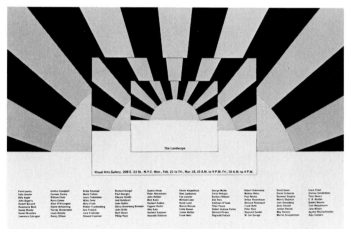

Poster for a survey of contemporary landscape painting designed by Milton Glaser. Courtesy Visual Arts Museum, New York

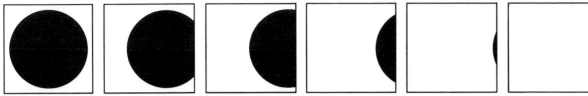

16

17

18

Pirelli Presenter-an articulated tyreman. Design by Pentagram Design Partnership, Courtesy Pirelli, LTD (GB)

Another position-change sequence that demonstrates rapid motion can be seen in Figure 19—a golf ball package designed for Hogan. This visual sequence is actually a combination of two types—an additive sequence and a position-change sequence. First, it is additive because the ball shape becomes progressively more distinct as weight is added sequentially to the lines. Second, it is a position-change sequence, since from left to right the position of the ball image changes in a progressive sequence.

## Metamorphic Sequence

A metamorphic sequence transforms one image into another. This transformation is caused by gradually subtracting visual characteristics from the shape or form of the first image while adding characteristics of the second. The metamorphosis continues until the visual identity of the first image is completely deleted and that of the second is completely assumed.

We can apply metamorphic sequences to any two- or three-dimensional pair of images. Smooth transition from one form to another can be achieved visually by transposing certain characteristics. Figure 20 is an example of a metamorphic sequence used to transform a simple circle into a square; Figure 21 demonstrates a more complex transformation caused by a metamorphic sequence that changes a star into a dollar sign. Stars are also used in the metamorphic sequence in Figure 22, but they are real stars that have been transformed into the CBS television trademark. And, in Figure 23—a direct mail piece to doctors on the subject of drug dependence—a metamorphic illustration has been used to transform a woman into a bottle of pills.

19

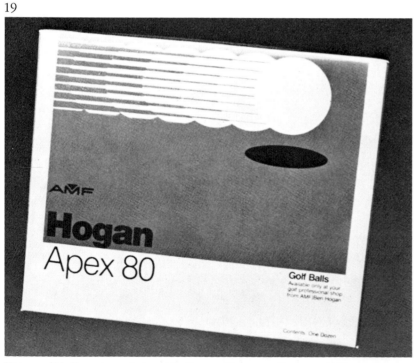

Hogan golf balls package designed by Eugene Grossman. Courtesy, AMF

20

21

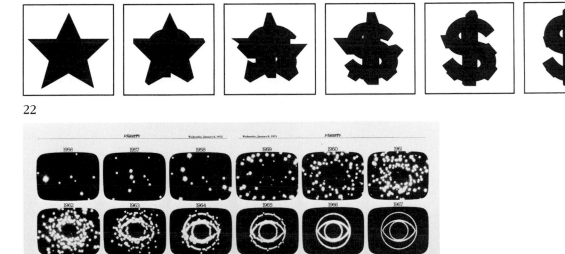

22

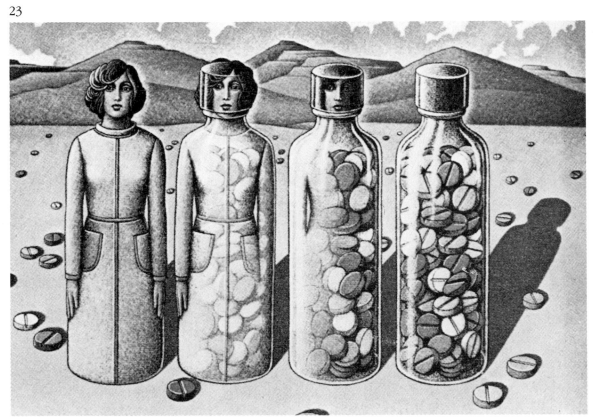

Fall campaign promotion advertisement,
Art Director: Lou Dorfsman, Designers:
Lou Dorfsman, Ted Andresalus. Courtesy CBS

Design for Smith Kline and French Labs by Roger Hane

### Distortion/Destruction Sequence

A distortion/destruction sequence deliberately distorts or destroys an image in a progressive sequence to communicate a change in appearance that has been caused by opposing forces.

Distortion/destruction sequences not only have great potential for communicating the effects of opposing forces, they also have the capacity to infer dynamic opposition without actually having to show the opponents. For example, the grid in Figure 24 is being progressively distorted by an invisible force. It appears that a force has punched a hole in the grid and is widening the hole so it can pass through it. In a similar way, the square shown in Figure 25 is progressively being destroyed by an unseen power. In both examples, as the viewer we are actively required to participate by speculating on the unseen forces; this type of participation can increase the excitement and effectiveness of the communication.

A specific application of a distortion/destruction sequence in a single frame of reference can be seen in Figure 26. In this example, a brochure cover for a drug manufacturer effectively communicates marital tension by progressively distorting from top to bottom a heart composed of squares. In Figure 27, an amusing distortion/destruction sequence is executed in multiple frames of reference. In this sequence, opposing forces are visually engaged in a conflict until finally one force overcomes and destroys the other in an unusual manner.

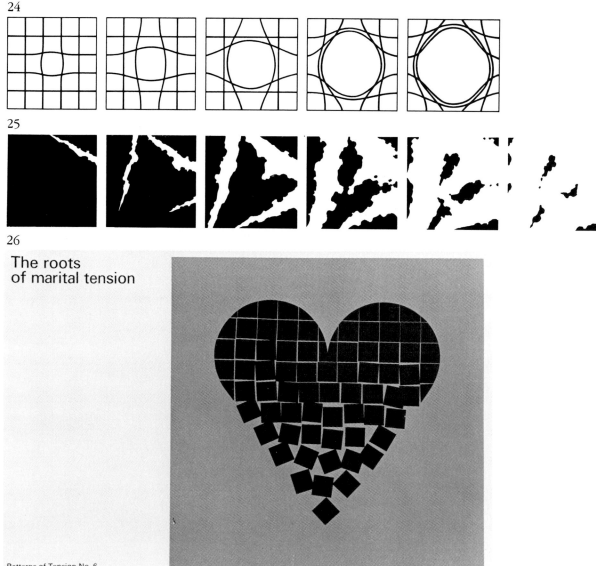

24

25

26

The roots
of marital tension

Patterns of Tension No. 6

Brochure cover designed by Gottschalk & Ash LTD for Roche. Courtesy Hoffman-La Roche LTD

## PIGMENTS

For anyone studying color as a property of pigment, a short discussion of the various pigments' differences and similarities may be useful. A *pigment* is a coloring agent that is insoluble. Pigments are usually produced in powder form and mixed with various binding agents, such as oil, gum, or wax to make inks, paints, and crayons. Wet media, like paint and ink, also utilize a solution or liquifying agent that acts as a carrier for the pigment and binder. Turpentine and water are the two solutions most commonly used for commercial wet media products. All commercially available pigment products, both wet and dry, use identical pigments. It is the various binders and solutions that determine the type of finished product. So in terms of color mixing and color relationships, the color properties of the various pigments are identical—only their working properties and methods of application vary.

| Contemporary dry pigments | Binders | Solution | Brief working properties |
|---|---|---|---|
| Colored pencils: | Wax and extreme pressure | None | Not easily mixed in use; thus limited to colors as they come from the crayon. |
| Wax crayons: | Bees wax or carnauba wax | None | Not easily mixed in use; thus limited to colors as they come from the crayon. |
| Chalk or pastel crayons: | Gum | None | Binders are weak and must be fixed with a spray fixative to prevent smudging. Colors are relatively easy to mix in use in order to alter color as it comes from the crayon. |
| Oil pastel crayons: | Linseed oil | None but soluble in turpentine | Easily mixed in use to alter color, easily smudged. Will never completely dry but can be coated with polyurethane to fix. |
| Conté crayons: | Linseed oil | None but soluble in turpentine | Easily smudged but can be fixed with any spray fixative. Only available in two colors—black and red brown. |

| Contemporary wet pigments | Binders | Solution | Brief working properties |
|---|---|---|---|
| Water color: also available in dry form | Gum, honey, glycerine | Water | Dries rapidly to the touch, but can be easily disolved again in water after drying. Large color selection easily mixed in use. Water color is transparent or translucent when dry. |
| Gouache: designers color | Gum honey, glycerine | Water | Very similar to water color except opaque when dry. Large selection of vivid colors easily mixed in use. |
| Casein: | Skimmed milk, acid | Water | Easily mixed in use. Opaque when dry. Almost insoluble in water when dry. Characteristic chalky look to color when dry. Dries fairly rapidly to the touch. |
| Tempera: also available in dry form | Milk, egg | Water | Characteristic chalky look to color when dry. Color strength is usually inferior due to proportion of filler to pigment. Easily mixed in use, dries rapidly, opaque, and water soluble when dry. |
| Oil paint and oil based printing ink: | Linseed oil | Turpentine | Easily mixed in use. Very wide range of color choice. Dries slowly to the touch—12 to 36 hours depending on color used and thickness of application. Opaque when dry but can be applied transparently if sufficiently thinned. Almost insoluble when dry. |
| Acrylic paint: | Acrylics and polymers (plastic) | Water | Easily mixed in use. Very wide range of color choice. Dries rapidly to the touch—5 to 10 minutes. Can be applied for opaque or transparent effects when dry. Very permanent and insoluble when dry. Dried color is actually a form of plastic. |

## CLASSIFICATION SYSTEMS: THE COLOR WHEEL

Colors are also knows as *hues*. Color names such as red, blue, and green, are verbal methods of identifying various colors. Naming color is one method of color classification. There are many other methods, and each is dependent on the purpose it is intended to serve: color matching, color marketing, color quality control, color mixing, number identification systems, and so on.

The most common and widely known classification is the wheel system. A variety of color wheels have been developed since they were introduced in the early 1700s. The best-known color wheels are shown in Figures 3, 4, and 5. All these wheel systems arrange colors in the same order as found in the spectrum. Because of its practical value, the twelve-part color wheel (Figure 5) is the most commonly used. A twelve-part color wheel that has been expanded to extend its practical application in color work can be seen in Figure 6. This color wheel can be used in much the same way that a calculator is used in mathematics. In the rest of this chapter, we will look at some of its uses.

4

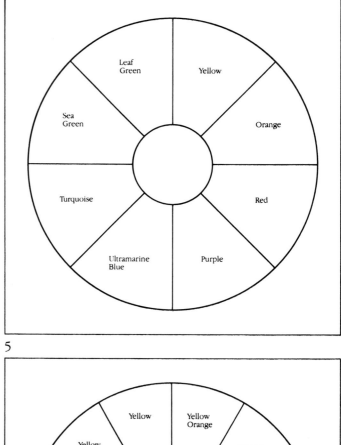

3

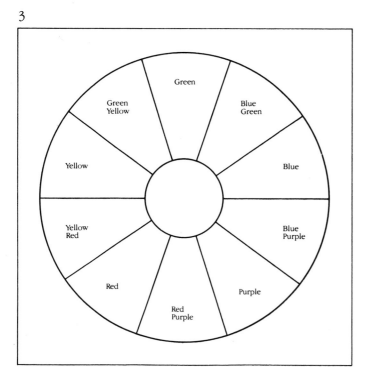

5

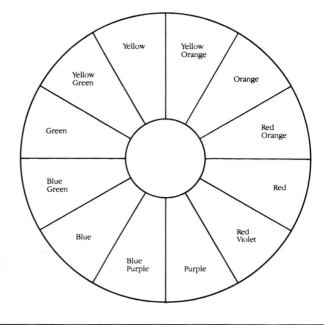

6

Expanded color wheel

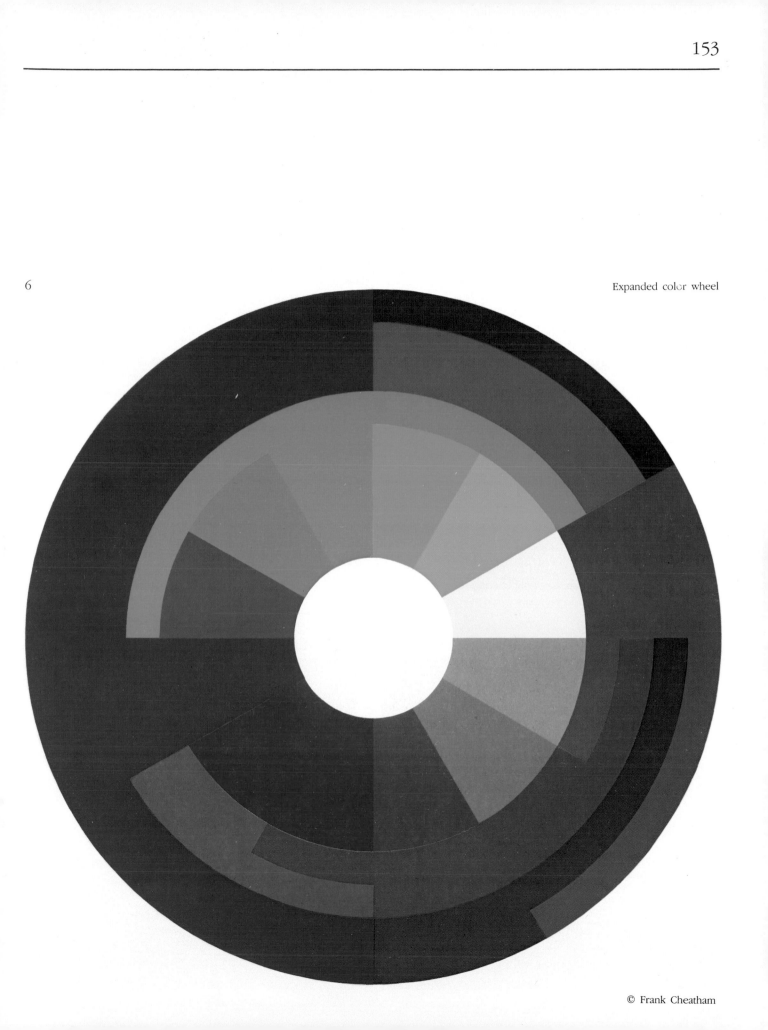

## NEUTRAL GRAYS

Because neutral gray is rarely found in nature, it can be seen as primarily a product of human invention. *Neutral gray results from mixing black and white pigments together in any proportion.* Therefore, it is possible for us to mix an almost unlimited number of different neutral grays by varying the amount of black added to white. In Figure 7, the neutral gray in the lefthand square of the diagram has a very light tonal quality because little black has been mixed with a relatively large amount of white. Conversely, the neutral gray in the righthand square has a very dark tonal quality because little white has been mixed with a relatively large amount of black. This light and dark tonal quality, or appearance, is referred to as *value.* All neutral grays have value, ranging from very light to very dark, depending upon the various proportions of white and black.

Neutral gray, since it has no discernible hue, is not considered to be a color. However, neutral gray is included in this discussion because in art it is frequently used with color, as well as mixed with other colors.

When neutral gray is mixed with a color, the resultant mixture creates another type of gray known as a *chromatic gray.*

## CHROMATIC GRAYS

The dictionary tells us that "chroma" is a Greek word meaning color; "chromatic" means containing color or colors. Consequently, a chromatic gray is simply *a gray that contains color.*

There are several ways to arrive at chromatic grays. One way has already been mentioned—adding a color to a neutral gray. If very small amounts of color are added to large amounts of neutral gray, the visual result is similar to the appearance of the neutral grays of the same value (Figure 8). In this example, the row of chromatic grays looks very neutral because the small amounts of color are diminished, or neutralized, by the large amount of neutral gray in each. However,

7

Light to dark tonal quality of neutral grays in nine steps

Neutral grays      8

Chromatic grays achieved by mixing small amounts of color with neutral grays

Chromatic grays made by mixing small amounts of neutral gray with colors      11

Colors with no neutral gray added to them

Red lightened in value by adding white is neutralized      9

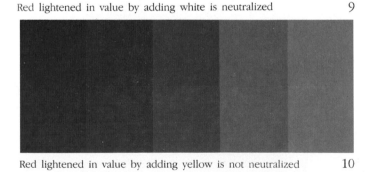

Red lightened in value by adding yellow is not neutralized      10

Blue darkened in value by adding purple is not neturalized      12

Blue darkened in value by adding black is neutralized

chromatic grays do not always have this very neutral appearance. If only small amounts of neutral gray are mixed with large amounts of color, the mixtures result in chromatic grays of an entirely different nature (Figure 11). These chromatic grays appear more colorful than neutral—in fact, the examples do not seem grayed or neutralized until they are compared with colors that have no neutral gray.

Another way by which colors can be neutralized, grayed, or transformed into chromatic grays involves the separate use of black or white. Certain colors become chromatic grays with the addition of any amount of white. Others become chromatic grays with the addition of any amount of black. In order to show how colors can become neutralized or grayed in this way, Figures 9 and 10 present two rows of red. The values in both rows of each color have been adjusted from light to dark so that each square corresponds in value to the one below. The values in the bottom row have been lightened by adding a color that is naturally lighter in value—in this

case, yellow. The values in the top row have been lightened by adding white. The colors on the top appear "washed out," neutralized, or grayed compared to those in the bottom row. In Figure 12, black has a similar neutralizing effect when added to blue to darken its value. Blue has been darkened in value with either purple or a darker tube blue in the top row, while black has been used in the bottom row. We can easily see that the blues in the bottom row. We can easily see that the blues in the bottom row are grayed in comparison to those on the top row. Finally, Figure 13 depicts the expanded color wheel, which shows the colors that can be transformed into chromatic grays by the addition of black or white, respectively.

Yet another way in which colors can be grayed down, neutralized, or transformed into chromatic grays involves mixing two or more complementary colors.

White added to any of these colors transforms them into chromatic grays

To lighten the values of these colors without neutralizing them, add a lighter value color from this group which is not a complement or near complement

Black added to any of these colors transforms them into chromatic grays

To darken their values without neutralizing them, add a darker value color from this group—or the group above—which is not a near complement

## COMPLEMENTS AND COMPLEMENTARY CHROMATIC GRAYS

*Complementary* colors are those that appear directly opposite one another on the twelve-part color wheel (Figure 14). When complementary colors are mixed in any proportion, they neutralize one another and create a chromatic gray. Figure 15 illustrates the various chromatic grays achieved by mixing each of the complementary pairs in equal proportions.

*Near complements* are another group of color pairs that, when mixed, react similarly to the complementary colors to create a series of somewhat less pronounced chromatic grays. Near complements are colors that are very close to being complementary but are not exactly opposite each other on the twelve-part color wheel. Figure 16 designates the near complements of blue-purple (yellow and orange). Figure 17 illustrates the near complements of blue (yellow-orange and red-orange) and so forth around the wheel. The near complements of blue (yellow-orange and red-orange) have enough orange components in each to cause a complementary neutralization when mixed with blue. Chromatic grays that result from mixing equal amounts of blue with an equal amount of yellow-orange and an equal amount of red-orange can be seen in Figure 18. Various chromatic grays will result from mixing other near complements.

**14**

Complementary colors are opposite one another on the color wheel

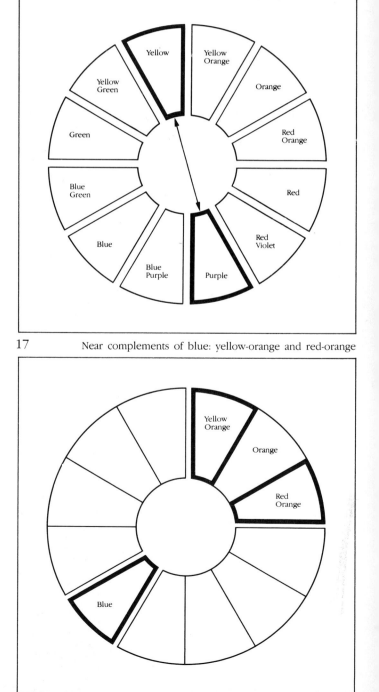

**16**  Near complements of blue-purple: yellow and orange

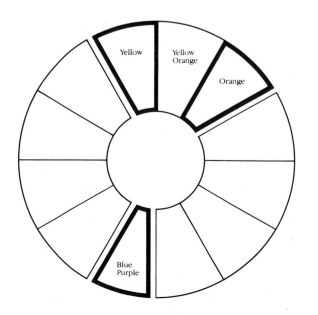

**17**  Near complements of blue: yellow-orange and red-orange

15

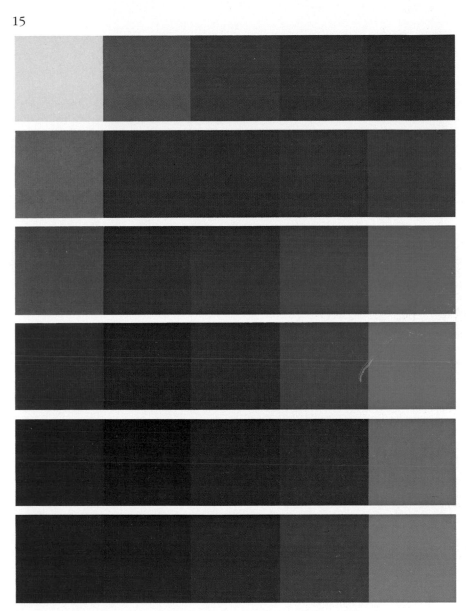

Complementary color pairs and the chromatic grays that result from their mixture

Chromatic grays resulting from mixing blue with its near complements                    18

Looking at the expanded color wheel, we can see a number of colors placed around the outside circumference of the twelve-part wheel (Figure 19). Any of these colors, when mixed with a color opposite it, either inside or outside the twelve-part wheel, will also create a variety of chromatic grays. For example, purple, the widest band of color on the outside color wheel, is opposite half the colors on the wheel. Therefore, the mixture of purple in varying proportions with any of the six colors opposite it on the twelve-part wheel and with any of the six colors opposite it on the outside wheel, will result in chromatic grays. In the same way, Figure 20 illustrates additional colors, such as

blue-green, raw umber, and olive green, and their near complements. Mixtures of these colors and their near complements in varying amounts will also yield a variety of rich chromatic grays.

Like neutral grays, chromatic grays and complementary chromatic grays have light and dark tonal qualities. Any chromatic gray or complementary chromatic gray can be lightened in value by adding white and darkened in value by adding black (Figure 21). In all cases, the addition of white or black to any chromatic gray will make it appear even more neutralized or grayed.

Near complements using the expanded color wheel

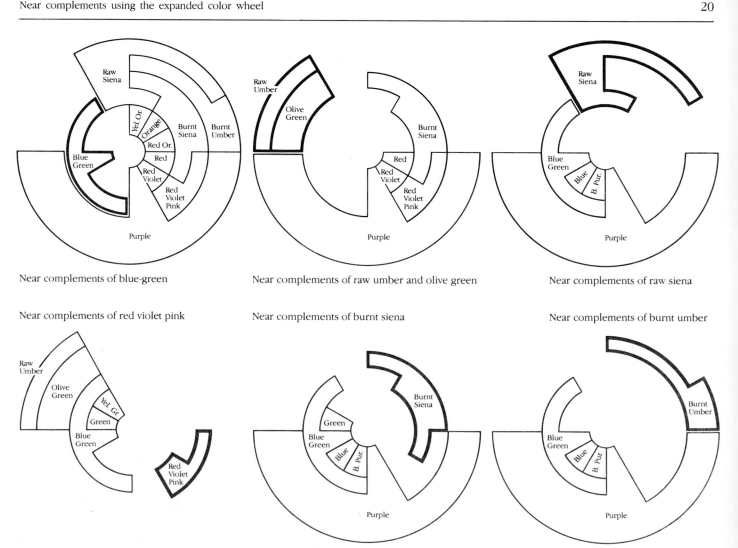

Near complements of blue-green

Near complements of raw umber and olive green

Near complements of raw siena

Near complements of red violet pink

Near complements of burnt siena

Near complements of burnt umber

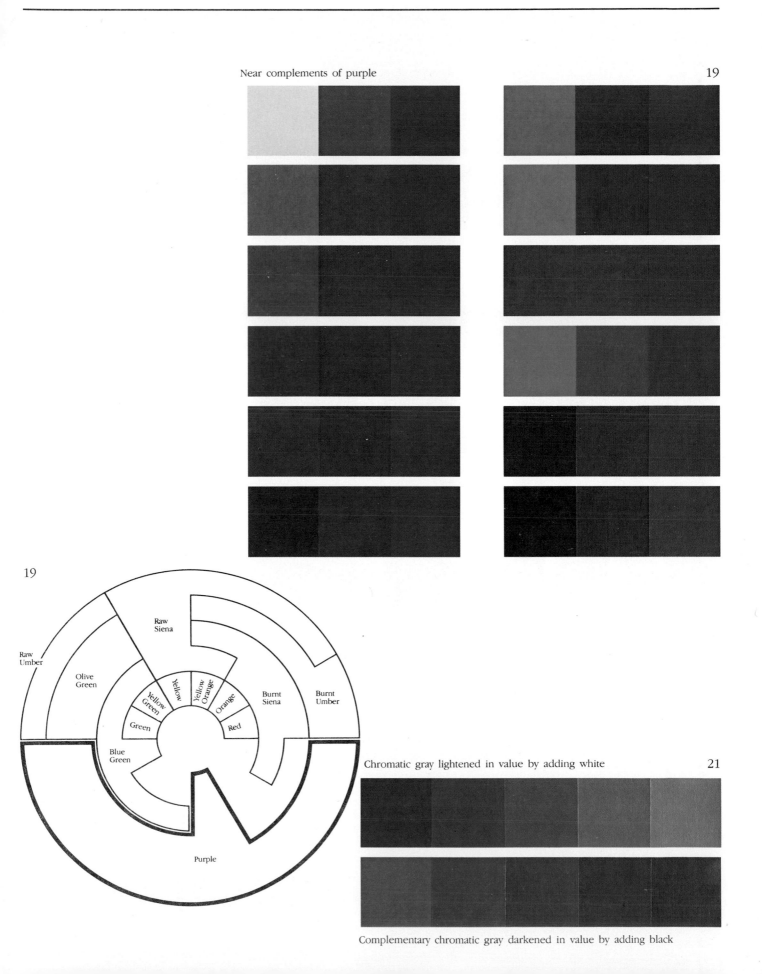

Near complements of purple 19

19

Raw
Siena

Raw
Umber

Olive
Green

Yellow
Green

Yellow

Yellow
Orange

Burnt
Siena

Burnt
Umber

Green

Orange

Red

Blue
Green

Purple

Chromatic gray lightened in value by adding white 21

Complementary chromatic gray darkened in value by adding black

22          Blue lightened in value by adding white

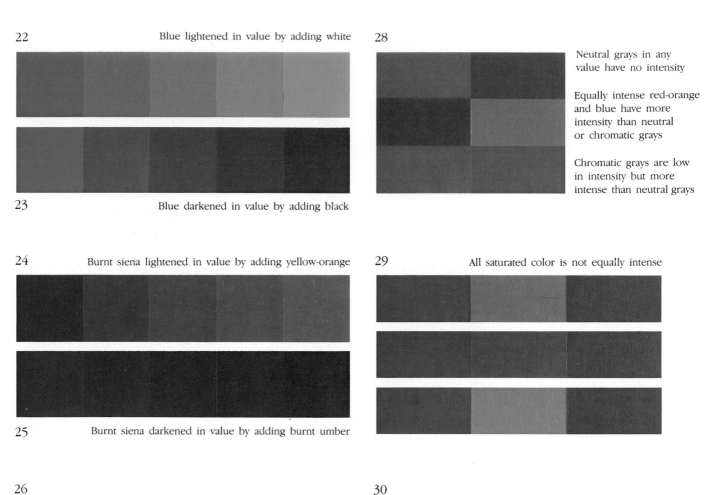

23          Blue darkened in value by adding black

28

Neutral grays in any value have no intensity

Equally intense red-orange and blue have more intensity than neutral or chromatic grays

Chromatic grays are low in intensity but more intense than neutral grays

24        Burnt siena lightened in value by adding yellow-orange

25        Burnt siena darkened in value by adding burnt umber

29        All saturated color is not equally intense

26

Colors of different value (left above) separate more than colors of equal value (right above)

30

Neutral grays, chromatic grays, complements or close complements mixed with any saturated color will always yield an unsaturated color mixture. Neutral gray mixture (top row center); chromatic gray mixture (bottom row center)

27

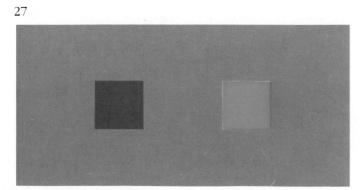

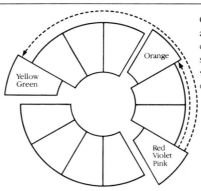

Colors of the same value and also close together on the color wheel, have less visual separation than those of the same value that are far apart on the color wheel

## VALUE

Color, like all tones of gray, has value—lightness and darkness. Logically, then, commercial color as it comes from the tube or container also has a value range from light to dark. This value range is an inherent characteristic of unaltered color derived from natural and synthetic pigments. Yellows, yellow-oranges, and oranges are naturally light in value. Purple, red-purple, and blue-purple are naturally dark in value. Yellow is the lightest color represented on the twelve-part color wheel and purple is the darkest. It is understood that yellow is not as light in value as white and that purple is not as dark in value as black. However, yellow and purple represent the light and dark value extremes in color, just as black and white represent those extremes in neutral grays.

The values of "tube" colors can be altered in various ways. We can lighten the value of any of these colors by adding white. Figure 22 illustrates blue progressively lightened in value by adding white. Similarly, we can darken the value of any color by adding black. The same blue darkened in value by adding black can be seen in Figure 23. Perhaps a less obvious way to alter the values of colors consists of adding a naturally lighter or darker color. For instance, since yellow-orange is naturally ligher in value than burnt sienna, it can be added to burnt sienna in order to lighten the value (Figure 24). Correspondingly, since burnt umber is naturally darker in value than burnt sienna, it can be added to burnt sienna to darken its value (Figure 25).

With practice, the values of colors and grays can be easily manipulated, and we can learn to anticipate the hue changes that will occur when altering values. Once this degree of proficiency is achieved, we can control the value patterns to achieve an intended effect. For instance, a great deal or very little value contrast in color may be desired. When using little value contrast, the visual separation between colored areas is dependent upon color change rather than value change. Conversely, the greater the value change, the greater the separation there will be between colors. Figure 26 illustrates this value and color separation principle. Raw umber and blue are distinctly different colors. When used together in their natural values, a great deal of value and color separation occurs between them; this can be seen on the left. On the extreme right, the blue has been darkened so that it is identical in value to the raw umber. In this way, it is possible to see that the separation in the example on the right is totally dependent on color change.

Finally, colors that are closely related in hue will have less separation visually than those that are not closely related in hue. For example, pink and orange are more closely related in hue than pink and green. As a result, less color separation occurs between pink and orange than between pink and green, even when all values are equal (Figure 27).

## INTENSITY AND SATURATION

*Intensity* simply refers to the brightness or dullness of a color or gray.

Sometimes there is confusion between the intensity of a color and the value of that same color. That is, it is not difficult for us to recognize that a yellow or red-orange, such as those found on the color wheel, are intense colors. However, colors such as purple or blue—as found on the color wheel—are not always identified as being as intense as red-orange or yellow. Actually, blue and purple *are* as intense as red-orange and yellow—the difference between the two groups is value. Obviously, blue and purple are darker in value than yellow or red-orange, but they are all of equal intensity. Therefore, we can see that the intensity of a color has little to do with its value, and that it is entirely possible for both dark and light colors to be intense.

Just as colors that are bright are called intense, those colors that are not bright are said to be of low intensity. For example, chromatic grays are most often perceived as low-intensity colors. And neutral grays have no intensity (Figure 28).

Intensity and saturation are also often confused. While the meanings of both, in reference to color, have a definite relationship, there is an important difference between the two. Intensity has been defined as the brightness of a color. *Saturation* refers only to the purity of a color, and not to its intensity. That is, many saturated colors are intense, while others are not. The distinction to be made, then, is this: All intense colors are saturated, but not all saturated colors are intense. For instance, in Figure 29, the earth colors, raw sienna and burnt sienna, used directly from the tube are saturated (pure). However when these are contrasted with yellow-orange, red-orange, even blue, neither appears very intense.

A number of things can affect the purity, or saturation, of colors. Mixing neutral or chromatic grays or a complementary color with any saturated color will result in an unsaturated color mixture (Figure 30). Additionally, as previously mentioned in the discussion of chromatic grays, any amount of white added to certain colors and any amount of black added to others will create an unsaturated color. Therefore, when the need arises to lighten or darken the value of a color while maintaining its saturation, a method other than adding black and white must be used.

On the expanded color wheel (Figure 31), the colors clockwise from green through red can be lightened in value while maintaining saturation by adding yellow or any other color from that group that is lighter in value. Figure 32 compares a very dark burnt umber that has been lightened in value by the addition of orange to one that has been lightened with white. Only the mixture of orange and burnt umber is saturated. All these colors (Figure 31) can be darkened in value, while maintaining saturation, by adding darker-value colors from the group or small amounts of black. In all these cases, slight color changes will take place.

The colors blue-green through red-violet, moving counterclockwise on the wheel in Figure 31, can be lightened in value while maintaining saturation by add-

ing white; however, they can only be darkened in value (maintaining saturation) by adding a darker-value color from the group. Blue-green is the one exception. In order to maintain saturation, it can only be darkened with another, darker blue-green. Figure 33 compares a saturated, medium-value blue-purple progressively darkened in value by the addition of a darker-value blue with one that has been darkened by the addition of black. Only the mixtures of the blue-purple and the darker-value blue appear saturated.

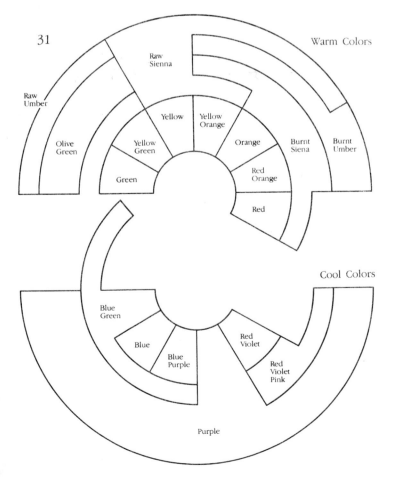

31

Warm Colors

Raw Sienna

Raw Umber

Yellow
Yellow Orange

Olive Green

Yellow Green

Orange

Burnt Siena

Burnt Umber

Green

Red Orange

Red

Cool Colors

Blue Green

Red Violet

Blue

Blue Purple

Red Violet Pink

Purple

These colors can be lightened in value while maintaining their saturation in only one way—by adding lighter value colors from this group which are not complements or near complements

Any white added to lighten the values of any of these colors will render them unsaturated

These colors can be darkened in value while maintaining saturation in two ways—by adding darker value colors from the group which are not complements or near complements and by adding small amounts of black (5% or less)

These colors can be darkened in value while maintaining their saturation in only one way—by adding darker value colors from this group which are not near complements (blue-green is a near complement of red-violet, red-violet pink and purple)

Any black added to any of the colors in this group renders them unsaturated

All the colors in this group can be lightened in value while maintaining saturation by adding up to approximately 75% white

A lighter value blue-green can be added to blue and blue-purple to lighten their value while maintaining their saturation. Any lighter value color, except blue-green, can be added to the other colors in the group to lighten their values while maintaining their saturation.

## WARM—COOL

Color has a curious characteristic that can be associated with weather, or temperature. Color can appear warm in feeling or cool in feeling. And, at times, it can even feel quite hot or cold. The various temperature feelings associated with color can be controlled and manipulated in a composition in the same ways that value, intensity, and saturation can be. For example, the color composition on the left in Figure 34 is composed entirely of warm colors. As a result, it feels quite warm and perhaps even uncomfortable—like being in a stuffy room. The composition to the right has been changed very little, except that a small amount of cool color has been introduced into the otherwise predominantly warm composition. Although this composition also feels warm, it has a fresher feeling—as though a window has been opened.

The expanded color wheel, Figure 31, shows those colors that usually appear warm and those that appear cool. Two colors—green and red-violet—are designated as transitional colors between warm and cool. In any given composition, the transitional colors can appear either warm or cool, depending on the colors surrounding them and their relative amounts. In most cases, however, green will appear warm and red-violet will appear cool. Color compositions are usually more successful if they contain both warm and cool components.

32
Burnt umber lightened in value with yellow-orange remains saturated

Burnt umber lightened in value with white is unsaturated

33
Blue-purple darkened in value with a darker blue remains saturated

Blue-purple darkened in value with black is unsaturated

34
Composition composed entirely of warm colors feels uncomfortably warm or stuffy

When a cool color is introduced into the composition, the colors —although still predominantly warm—feel fresher, less oppressive

35

All light browns in the top row are identical in color, value, intensity and degree of warmness. All appear identical because they are surrounded by white

All light browns in this row are identical to those in the top row although they now appear different to those in the top row and to one another

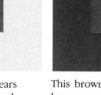

This brown appears to be darker in value than the others

This brown appears to have a greenish cast and seems more intense than the others

This brown appears more yellow and lighter in value than the others

36

Warm and cool colors different in value and intensity

Warm and cool colors close in value but different in intensity

Warm and cool colors close in intensity but different in value

37

Color relationships which seem unpleasant or ugly

Identical colors adjusted by amount now appear unusual but not ugly

## COLOR INTERACTION AND AMOUNT RELATIONSHIPS

When colors touch, without being separated by any black or white, they often alter or modify one another's visual character. Such a relationship between two or more colors is called *color interaction*. At times, colors can undergo such a change in character that the difference is remarkable. Figure 35 illustrates identical colors of the same value placed on different background colors. When surrounded by white, the browns appear identical—which they are. However, when the same browns are adjacent to the various background colors without a white division, the character of each brown is noticeably altered. An additional change also takes place each time the background color changes. Even though each brown is identical, some appear lighter or darker in value as well as more or less intense than their neighbors. A hue change is only one method of varying the interaction between colors.

Value, intensity, saturation, and warm-cool adjustments can also be used to create different interactions of color. For example, Figure 36 varies the color interaction between a warm and a cool color by altering the degree of value and intensity contrast. As the colors become closer in both value and intensity, there is a more lively and active interaction between them.

Another factor that can radically alter the visual character of a color composition is *amount relationship*. By increasing or decreasing the relative area of a color, the amount relationship between colors will be changed. When this occurs, the overall character of the color composition also changes. Any combination of colors—no matter how awful they may appear initially—can be made to work satisfactorily by adjusting the various amounts of color relative to one another. For instance, in Figure 37 two color compositions have been made with colors of the same hue, value, saturation, and intensity. The combination of colors in the composition on the top seems unpleasant and ugly. The same colors in the composition on the bottom appear unusual and exciting. This change in visual character is the result of increasing and decreasing the amounts of each color used. Obviously, when working with color the ability to adjust amount relationship is an indispensable tool. Amount relationships can easily be checked or changed by using one of the cropping procedures explained in Chapter 1.

## USING COLOR EFFECTIVELY

Two methods are helpful in learning to use color effectively. One way—the most important—is to use it often. The more we use it, the better we become. It is essential to know the color vocabulary and understand what each color term means. With practice, color manipulation and control can be acquired. In this way, visual expressions of great clarity and strength can be created.

The second way to learn to use color effectively is facilitated by the first method, and the two used in tandem can accelerate the effective color usage. The second method consists of studying and analyzing the manner in which other artists have used color. Many artists are proficient in color use, but the extraordinary colorists in art history are the most profitable to study. Paul Klee, Henri Matisse, Pierre Bonnard, Claude Monet, and Richard Lindner are a few of the great artists whose color usage, we suggest, is worthy of close examination.

SECTION TWO

10

COMMUNICATION

As individuals, we all possess a wide range of opinions, experiences, ideas, knowledge, and information. We all also have a basic need to exchange and share some of these thoughts and feelings with other people. This basic human need to transmit messages is called *communication.*

Communication can take many different forms. Much of our daily communication is based on the understanding of words that make up our language. Similarly, music, noises, sounds, and so on can act as verbal transmitters of thoughts and feelings. In combination with the verbal forms of communication, visual forms can be used to enhance or supplement the transmission of messages. Verbal stories printed visually in a book, pictures with captions, and dialogue that is acted, are all examples of visual-verbal combinations. And just as verbal communication can occur alone, visual communication can also function by itself. Symbols, photographs, emblems, and so on can all communicate thoughts and feelings.

It is this last form—the visual—that is most frequently associated with communication in art. However, in actuality all these forms, individually or in any number and variety of combinations, have been and are used by artists of every conceivable type and kind. Since ancient people first molded fertility charms out of wet clay and painted pictures on the walls of caves, artists have been among society's most important communicators. Actors, architects, composers, designers, musicians, painters, sculptors, all make significant and lasting contributions as a result of their desire to communicate an idea effectively. (See Figs. 1–8 for examples of communication in art.)

1,2,3. These residences in southern California designed by Irving Gill illustrate how emotional communication occurs in architecture. All these spaces feel warm, inviting, secure, and delightful as a result of the skillful manipulation of light, space, scale, texture, and pattern.

1

*Irving Gill;* Los Angeles County Museum in collaboration with The Art Center in La Jolla, Designer Louis Danziger, Photographer, Marvin Rand

## REQUIREMENTS FOR COMMUNICATION

For any communication to occur between human beings, it is essential that all those involved share some common information or knowledge. For instance, no intellectual verbal communication can take place between people unless they speak a common language or have an interpreter who speaks the languages involved. Similarly, no emotional communication can occur between people unless they have a background of common emotional information. Someone who does not know the meaning of a smile would not, without any further clues, respond to it as a gesture indicating friendliness or pleasure.

In the same way, for an artist to transmit a message to a viewer, some common information—conscious and/or intuitive—must exist. The artist's expression must reveal recognizable clues or suggest understandable qualities to the viewer if a response is to be obtained. Of course, every work cannot communicate to every possible viewer; but certain factors can help to maximize the communicative potential in a work. We will look more closely here at these elements and their functions.

2

*Irving Gill;* Los Angeles County Museum in collaboration with The Art Center in La Jolla, Designer Louis Danziger, Photographer Marvin Rand

3

*Irving Gill;* Los Angeles County Museum in collaboration with The Art Center in La Jolla, Designer Louis Danziger, Photographer Marvin Rand

## COMPONENTS OF COMMUNICATION IN ART

One area to consider is that of self-communication. Any artist, regardless of the mode of expression, is involved, to one degree or another, in a communication with self. Through an introspective process of conceptual, personal clarification, the artist may isolate and identify available information—both intellectual and emotional—that is pertinent to the idea to be communicated. It is both necessary and valuable for an artist, whether student or professional, to perform the exercise of mental articulation and clarification in order to ensure a clear and definite outward communication. More simply, this means that external communication will only be as clear and concise as that which has taken place on the self-communication level.

In addition to formal design processes such as light, scale, texture, the graphic designer uses words, images and symbols to reinforce his intended emotional, intellectual or emotional/intellectual communication to a mass audience.

4. The image of a criminal committing an unlawful act—removing a mattress tag—while a frightened but otherwise unharmed female watches, makes a strong and humorous statement about society's attitudes toward law and crime.

5. The verbal communication, *The Ascent of Man,* is reinforced by the composite image of men from various periods of history.

6. The swastika symbol used by the Nazis during World War II, commanded a response of fear and horror. That content has been changed by the designer's presentation of the symbol as a piece of chocolate candy. This new symbol is intended to communicate reparations in Germany after the war.

4

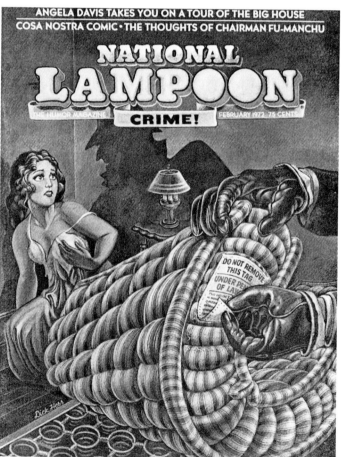

Cover for *National Lampoon,* Illustrated by Richard Hess

The ways and means of self-communication are infinite; they range from the specific to the abstract, from conscious awareness to unconscious awareness in both thinking and feeling. And, while self-communication is accomplished in ways best suited to the individual artist, there are three major aspects of communication that must usually be considered.

The artist uses the process of self-communication to determine *what* is to be communicated (content), *how* it is to be communicated (form), and *to whom* it is to be communicated (audience).

Depending upon how obvious or obscure, general or specific, direct or indirect, the artist wants the communication to be, the types of pertinent information—both emotional and intellectual—can be adjusted to best communicate the message. For example, if we wanted to communicate urgency in a primarily emo-

tional way, a single scream might accomplish this. Or if a purely intellectual communication of urgency was needed, simply saying the word "Help" could transmit the message. However, if a scream simultaneously forms the word "Help," a more specific and stronger communication of urgency would occur. In the same way, as artists we can control the communication potential of what we wish to express by adjusting, modifying, and emphasizing the emotional and intellectual information. (It should be noted that in reality neither intellectual nor emotional communication is ever transmitted solely by itself. However, in order to understand their use in various expressions, it is easier to categorize them as being distinctly independent or specifically combined.)

5

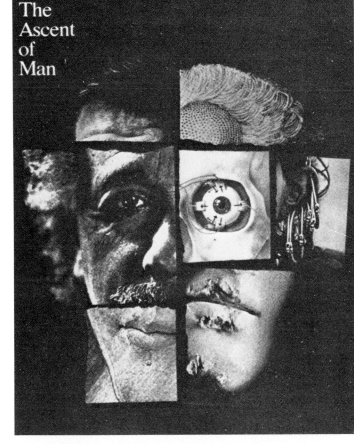

Poster designed by Chermayeff & Geismar Associates, Courtesy Mobil Oil Corporation

6

Book jacket designed by Milton Glaser

After determining what the content of the communication should be, the artist can transmit the message in one or any combination of the three forms we have discussed: visual, verbal, or visual-verbal. Again, as artists, how we use these methods of communication depends upon what we are trying to say and to whom we want to say it.

Since different kinds of artists attempt to communicate to varied audiences on multiple levels, consideration of the size and educational background of the intended audience can be a key factor. For example, it is difficult for an end product of an architect's creative expression—a building—to communicate to a mass audience of varied backgrounds on anything but an emotional level, since little common intellectual information is shared. The architect must work with those elements (scale, light, sound, form, texture) that are capable of producing the strongest emotional impact. In comparison, a graphic designer who can work with a greater number of visual and verbal elements (words,

images, symbols) and with all types of content has more communication opportunities than an architect. A filmmaker has still greater communicative potential when trying to reach a large, varied audience, since the very common information of motion and sound can be incorporated into the final expression.

Finally, when a work of art is completed, its elements (content and form) will be communicated to and considered by the intended audience. If the viewer responds on either a conscious/intellectual or intuitive/emotional level, then the artist has accomplished the intended goal, namely, communication and response.

As artists, we can acquire an understanding of communication informally, but it is possible—and perhaps more expedient—to learn and practice many elements of communication formally. The next two chapters present formal methods of obtaining a better understanding of communication.

7. To communicate the content of this book, both historical and contemporary symbols have been used. The ink bottle, quill pen and handwritten script are representative of historical writings. The collaged cut-out execution of these symbols is contemporary. Finally, all of these have been combined with the British seal to communicate the title's entire message, *Forces in Modern British Literature 1885–1956.*

8. The image of a black man with part of the American flag imprinted on his face graphically communicates a certain part of American society. In this way, the visual communication is used to strengthen the verbal communication, *Of Black America.*

7

Book cover, *Forces in Modern British Literature 1885–1956;*
William York Tindall. Designed by Paul Rand, (c) Alfred A. Knopf, Inc.

8    Advertisement for CBS News: Black America. Art Director: Lou Dorfsman, designed for CBS Television Network

*THE NEW YORK TIMES, TUESDAY, JULY 2, 1968*

Tonight, in the first of a seven-part series broadcast on Tuesdays in the coming weeks, CBS News tries to set the record straight to help close some of the gaps of understanding that separate black and white America.

In tonight's broadcast, Bill Cosby, actor and comedian, guides us through a history of the attitudes that have distorted the image of the Negro in America. He shows how those attitudes were formed and what they have done to us. He shows the black man's need to know who he is and what happens to him when he cannot find the answer.

On succeeding Tuesdays, Of Black America will present a study of the Negro soldier, a conference of black American and African leaders, a public opinion survey of black and white attitudes, a look at what the black American has contributed to sports and music, a history of slavery, and an examination of African life and civilization through the eyes of three young black Americans.

Sponsored by Xerox Corporation, with Perry Wolff as Executive Producer, Of Black America presents the Negro in a new light, with balance and perspective. If it helps both black and white Americans to understand each other a little better, if it helps to change some of their attitudes toward each other, it will prove to be one of the most rewarding series ever presented on television.

### First of a seven-part series

### "Black History; Lost, Stolen or Strayed."

America has camouflaged the black man. For three hundred years the attitudes of white Americans to black and black Americans to white have been subjected to misunderstandings, erasures and distortions damaging to both. The black American's achievements have been misplaced, his contributions obscured. He has been told so often who he is not that he no longer knows who he is. And the frustrations of his search for identity and recognition underlie much of today's crisis of alienation in American society.

# OF BLACK AMERICA

## 10 TONIGHT CBS NEWS ◉ 2

# SECTION TWO

# 11

IDEA

To better understand the concept of "idea," we can separate it into several fundamental elements and then analyze each one individually. This makes it possible for us to explore and establish personal interpretations and methods of application in relation to ideas. "Idea" awareness, interpretation, exploration, and execution is essential to the creation of works of art that possess quality and integrity.

The approach of every experienced artist to having and developing ideas is ultimately different, since each controls what is more or less important in relation to the created work. For the beginning artist, though, at first it may be beneficial to practice a seemingly stringent analytical approach to learning, understanding, and applying ideas. This methodical practice will eventually result in the development of a unique, individual way of recognizing, formulating, and controlling ideas and expressions.

## THE ROLE OF IDEA IN ART

Since communication, on one level or another, is one of the primary functions of art, every form of art must begin with an idea or concept. Artists who have an understanding of the significance of the role of idea in art are more apt to create effective and successful expressions. It logically follows, then, that to communicate fully and convincingly to an audience, a complete working knowledge of the term "idea" is desirable.

## UNDERSTANDING AND RECOGNIZING IDEAS

The ability to generate ideas is the essential quality that separates human beings from all other animals. Ideas are the basis for all human achievements. Although we know very little scientifically about ideas—where they come from, how they occur, why they seem to come more easily to some people than to others—all of us are quite capable of having, defining, and using ideas.

Everyone has ideas and comes into contact with them every day in many forms. The *American Heritage Dictionary of the English Language* defines an idea as: 1. A mental representation forming an object of thought. 2. A product of thought as: a. an option, b. a plan or method, c. a notion; a fancy. 3. The gist or purpose of something. It may seem difficult to grasp what constitutes an idea because it has so many different meanings. However, for us as artists there will be less confusion if we ignore all but the first definition, "An idea is a *mental* representation forming an object of thought." It is this meaning which really applies to those engaged in creating visual art that is intended to communicate.

The development of an idea as a mental representation forming an object of thought begins with thinking—the process used to create an idea. This process can occur *only* in the brain. Consequently, even though as artists we are visually oriented, we cannot begin our process of visualization until a certain amount of previous thinking—no matter how minimal it might be—has been performed: *Visualization is the result of an idea, not an idea in itself.*

### Confusing Idea with Media/Process

Not being restricted in terms of media or process by professional dictates or cultural conditioning is an important part of the freedom in contemporary art. The contemporary artist has discovered what a great many primitives have always known—art which is magical can be created from anything that best communicates the intent. To those same primitive people, material and process are the least important aspects of their art. The message is plain—it takes more than process or media to create art.

It is not unusual for art students to fall into the mental trap of confusing "idea" with process or media. Media and process exploration have a definite place in the developmental growth of every artist. However, in work that is entirely based on process or media, process or media is frequently all there is; no message is ever delivered. It is wise to remember that media and process are only the messengers, not the message itself.

As a result of a heavy emphasis on media and process, confusion in relation to ideas may occur in one of the following ways:

1. *Assigning concept properties to visual characteristics.* Example: Red is not an idea; it is a verbal designation of a visual characteristic—color.

2. *Assigning concept properties to tactile characteristics.* Example: Smooth is not an idea; it is a verbal designation of a tactile characteristic—surface.

3. *Assigning concept properties to materials.* Example: Clay is not an idea; it is a verbal designation of a material.

4. *Assigning concept properties to process.* Example: Drawing is not an idea; it is a verbal designation of a process.

All the above—color, surface, material, and process— can be used to express, implement, or help communicate ideas. But, they are not ideas in themselves; they are merely the physical manifestations of ideas.

Another kind of confusion is mistaking *criteria*—information such as specifications, principles, and limitations—about a problem for the ideas needed to solve it. A criterion is not an idea.

These confusions cause us to forget the fact that an idea is a *mental* representation forming an object of *thought*. Ideas are nonsensory: they cannot be seen, touched, tasted, heard, or smelled. Our senses are able to come in contact only with the *results* of ideas once they have been materially produced or communicated.

## "IDEA MYSTERY" IN ART

Sometimes, in the visual arts, a kind of mystery surrounds "idea"—both its existence and its discussion. It is true that there are valid times and reasons for not discussing ideas, but more often than not, it is better *not* to shroud ideas in a cloak of mysterious silence. The following are some examples of valid and invalid uses of the "idea mystery." These examples attempt to do away with some of the confusion that may have been experienced at one time or another from the discussion of, or refusal to discuss, ideas.

One instance where the "idea mystery" is used frequently is in emotional communication. In many cases, it may be realistic for us not to discuss an idea when working principally with emotion. (Keep in mind that this applies only to emotional communication, never intellectual). For example, an artist's primary intent may be to obtain a response from an audience on any emotional level. There may be minimal concern that the audience understand exactly the artist's idea. The artist is interested only in stimulating an emotionally positive, individual response to the work. An explanation of the particular idea might interfere with this type of response, so it seems valid that the idea should remain a mystery. However, when the intent of the artist is to communicate a specific, emotional message and this message is not received, then the artist has failed to communicate. If that is the case, it does not mean that an aura of mystery should be created to disguise the original idea or lack of idea.

The fear of exposing something fragile, vulnerable, or magical about an idea that could be destroyed by verbal intrusiveness is another reason for not openly discussing an idea. We may feel that an idea in the infant stage can be seriously weakened by verbalization before it has had a chance to grow and become strong enough to survive revelation.

This is a valid reason for a serious, experienced artist not to verbalize an idea; it is not a valid reason for covering up weak or superficial ideas. And it is never an excuse for a beginning artist who is just learning to formulate and clarify concrete ideas. It is helpful for a beginning artist to verbalize even the vaguest, embryonic idea so that clear idea development can be practiced. When a level of proficiency in formulating ideas has been reached, a decision can be made concerning when it is appropriate or inappropriate to talk about ideas.

## WHERE IDEAS HAPPEN

Just as everyone has different physical characteristics, the most effective thinking environment for each individual person can be uniquely different. For example, a place conducive to thought for some people may be one with few distractions. Music, traffic noises, or even a conversation close by are examples of what might be considered distractions, but even these tend to vary with each individual. In the same way, we all seem to have times and/or places in which ideas come more easily to us. Examples of these times and/or places might be these: when taking a shower, driving a car, immediately after waking, or right before falling asleep. Realizing where and when this particular state occurs for each of us is an important self-discovery. There is a sense of security in knowing that even the most complex thinking can be tackled in this discovered personal environment. Many people also develop methods to alter their external physical environment by minimizing distractions. This allows them greater proficiency when they are thinking in these environments.

In addition to recognizing the external factors that discourage or encourage ideas, human beings can develop patterns of behavior that can help generate ideas. With information about the personal distractions that discourage and the behavior patterns that encourage more proficient thinking, we have the capacity to control how, where, and when ideas happen best for us.

## ACQUIRING IDEAS

Popular misconceptions die hard, and one of these lingering misconceptions is that the ability to think is very difficult, and for this reason it is the exclusive property of a very gifted minority. This is not true. We all are not only *capable* of thinking, we all actually *do* think in some form or another every moment of our lives. Consequently, inability to think is not the real issue; the actual issues to be dealt with concern the quality of thought and the disciplining of the thought processes.

Over a long period of time, anyone can develop, nurture, and accept popular misconceptions about thinking. Negative conditioning, whether in the home or school, at business or in the world at large, can play a dominant role in reinforcing these misconceptions.

Chances are that at one time or another all of us have been told, "You're not thinking." Since the mind is constantly active, the comment cannot be taken literally. Unfortunately, this negative comment is frequently accepted as fact. So, if children or adults are told often enough that they do not think, they soon begin to feel they are incapable of concentrating and unable to ac-

cept and comprehend new information. Such negative conditioning sows the seeds of an insecurity that eventually breeds a terrible frustration.

Another outcome born of frustration is concluding that there must be only one "right" answer, with an infinite number of "wrong" ones; and that the single "right" answer is extremely elusive. Again, this notion is nonproductive. In fact, usually there are many appropriate answers for any given situation. And it seems more reasonable that these answers should be formulated by the individual, rather than by acceptance of some predetermined answer from an outside source. Unfortunately, many people continually accept an external "right" answer instead of having faith in their own conclusions or opinions. As a result, these people feel that since they are constantly "wrong" and others "right," they must be incapable of actually thinking for themselves.

Fear of ideas and idea ownership are two more misconceptions about thinking. Some people are so uncomfortable with their own capabilities that if an idea should assert itself, they immediately conclude one of two things. Either their idea must be a poor one or, because they have one so rarely, any recognized idea must be jealously guarded for fear that it might be "stolen" and someone else will take credit for it. These people are also reticent to accept an idea from an outside source, because that source is thought to be the rightful "owner" of the idea. Such a belief is foolish. Ideas are plentiful and they belong to everyone until one is personalized by an individual's exploration, application, and implementation. And an unwillingness to accept ideas can slow down or paralyze the exchange of ideas, the stimulation of fresh ideas, and the acquisition of new and sometimes vital data. Acceptance and exploration of ideas from outside sources is in no way dishonest. As a matter of fact, if all people were constantly to reject information and ideas from others, human progress and growth would be negligible.

Another misconception about thinking concerns recall of factual data. This type of thinking demands only the unqualified regurgitation of facts. Obviously, recall can be a useful form of thought when the occasion demands, but it severely limits independent thought. Other forms of thought, such as philosophical or intuitive, are equally important, as the artist comes to realize when a logical process must be used in order to define and then creatively solve a problem.

These examples are but a few of the many kinds of nonproductive conditioning which reinforce the myth that thinking is the exclusive property of a gifted few. Society, whether intentionally or unintentionally, has conditioned a very large number of people to obey rules, follow instructions, and not ask questions unless they pertain to the rules or instructions. Fortunately, this situation is not irreversible. It is never too late for any of us to acknowledge our own innate ability to think. Acquiring information by research and storing several types of important data are just the first steps in discovering the ease and excitement of thinking for oneself. Also, by taking advantage of every opportunity to practice disciplined thinking, confidence in this ability can increase quickly.

## INFORMATION—
## THE COMPONENTS OF THOUGHT

Information can be briefly defined as stored or acquired knowledge on various subjects. However, for a more thorough understanding, we can classify information into four basic categories: factual, emotional, experiential, and specialized. These four types of information or data, whether newly or previously acquired, are the components of thought necessary to every living individual from the time of birth to the moment of death.

The first of these four types of information is *factual data* (Figure 1). It designates knowledge that exists, and is supported by evidence in reality. Mathematics, chemistry, and language are examples of factual data. *Emotional data* (Figure 2) includes the information acquired through experience and the senses that relates to feelings, such as anger, pain, joy. *Experiential data* (Figure 3), the third category, is the body of knowldge acquired from experiencing events in life. Independence, leadership, and confidence are examples of experiential data. This category also encompasses skills learned by observation and repetition. The fourth

| FACTUAL DATA | | 1 |
|---|---|---|

Acquired, Stored, or Obtainable Data Related to:

| | | |
|---|---|---|
| Philosophy | Logic | Mathematics |
| Engineering | Psychology | Language Geography |
| Physics | Astronomy | Geology |
| Demography | History | Marketing |
| Paleontology | Business | Botany |
| Research | Chemistry | Economics |
| Zoology | Sociology | Religion |
| Literature | Biology | Etc. |
| Grammar | Anthropology | |

| EMOTIONAL DATA | | 2 |
|---|---|---|

Acquired, Stored, or Obtainable Data Related to:

| | | |
|---|---|---|
| Sensitivity | Joy | Pain |
| Hate | Fear | Comfort |
| Independence | Dependence | Discomfort |
| Anxiety | Excitement | Sex |
| Touch | Confidence | Intuition |
| Insecurity | Love | Sorrow |
| Stress | Apprehension | Sensuality |
| Smell | Taste | Etc. |

| EXPERIENTIAL DATA | 3 |
|---|---|

Acquired, Stored, or Obtainable Data Related to:

| | |
|---|---|
| Behavioral Psychology | Problem Solving |
| Areas of Disinterest | Areas of Interest |
| Public Speaking | Customs |
| Language | Learning |
| Leadership | Insecurity |
| Seeing | Recalling |
| Maturity | Performing |
| Confidence | Etc. |

Preference Related to:

| | |
|---|---|
| food | music |
| style | dress |
| visual art | drama |
| fashion | etc. |

and final category is *specialized data* (Figure 4). This is the body of knowledge that usualy corresponds to an individual's vocation or avocation. An artist's drawing and design knowledge would be classified as specialized information.

Information in each of these four categories comes from two distinct sources. The first is previously acquired and stored data that can be immediately drawn upon and applied. The other source is used to supplement stored data and is generally referred to as *research*. Research can be done in numerous ways and places—at a museum or a library, in a playground—any place that allows a person to discover, observe, and question.

Both sources, and all four types of information, are essential to an individual's total thinking —or cognitive—process.

---

**SPECIALIZED DATA OF THE FINE ARTIST**     4

Acquired, Stored, or Obtainable Data Related to:

**Problem Solving**
Knowledge and ability to:
— think philosophically encompassing both the rational and the emotional.
— generate, direct, and organize ideas and thoughts.
— acquire mental processes for facilitating imagination and logic.
— pose concepts related to need for expression.
— ask and answer pertinent questions.
— order priorities.
— recall factual, emotional, and experiential data.
— intuit communication value of a variety of visual, emotional, and intellectual stimulants.
— make esthetic and philosophical judgments.
— research, recall, and use data related to concept.

**Process**
Knowledge in and ability to effectively apply:
— design philosophy and principles (gestalt, line, space, shape, volume, mass/void, contrast, repetition, change, time, motion, color, etc.) to transmit a desired idea and/or elicit a desired response from the viewer.
— skills necessary in creating the visual expression and an awareness of those skills that will most successfully accomplish the desired goal.

**Tools/Materials**
Skills and craftsmanship in:
— the basic tools of visual expression (pencils, paints, pens, brushes, canvas, papers, etc.).
— handling tools related to specific areas of interest, i.e., painting, printmaking, ceramics, sculpture, etc.
— use of basic and relevant hand or power tools.
— use of any relevant mechanical aids (cameras, Xerox machines, projection equipment, etc.).
— inventive use of various art and non-art materials and methods.

**Applied Arts/Architecture/Crafts**
Knowledge and ability to use:
— various media processes in both the two- and three-dimensional expressions of the above.
— the understanding of the similarities and differences between the fine arts and the above.
— the nature of the questions and demands (internal and external) with which each of the above must deal.
— the above as an area of research and understanding to ensure continued personal growth.

**History of Art/Design/Architecture**
Knowledge and ability to:
— recall and understand historical or current concepts, works, movements, and philosophies by individual and/or groups of artists, designers, architects.
— recall and understand the cultural climates, value systems, and societies that produced any movement, concept, and work.

## SPECIALIZED DATA OF THE GRAPHIC DESIGNER/APPLIED ARTIST 4

Acquired, Stored, or Obtainable Data Related to:

### Problem Solving
Knowledge and ability to:
— think philosophically encompassing both the rational and emotional.
— generate, direct, and organize ideas and thoughts.
— acquire mental processes for facilitating imagination and ideas.
— define and analyze problems relevant to need.
— ask and answer pertinent questions.
— order priorities.
— recall factual, emotional, and experiential data.
— intuit client and consumer response.
— acknowledge diverse value systems within the client/consumer context.
— make marketing decisions and esthetic judgments.
— recall and use data related to mass communication in design media, advertising media.
— verbalize clearly and succinctly any (or more) of the above when necessary.
— know the difference between a solution and a concept.

### Process
Knowledge in and ability to effectively apply:
— design philosophy and principles (gestalt, line, space, shape, volume, contrast, repetition, time, change, motion, color, etc.) to direct the desired or required emotional and intellectual response from the viewer.
— skills necessary in creating the visual communicative statement and an awareness of those skills that will most successfully accomplish the desired goal.
— typography in a sensitive, meaningful way that is most appropriate for the content of the communication.

### Tools/Materials
Skills and craftsmanship in:
— drawing, rendering, pencils, pens, ink, ruling pens, dyes, various papers and paper boards, paints, brushes, airbrushes, felt tip markers, matt board, drafting equipment, cameras, photo processing, and projection equipment.
— direct and mechanical transfer aids—Lucigraph, Art-O-Graph, Xerox machines, photostats, shading sheets, press-on letter forms, etc., and inventive use of various materials and methods.
— production techniques, materials related to client presentations, finished art, printing processes, etc.

### Fine Art Studio
Knowledge and ability to use:
— various media processes in both two- and three-dimensional expressions.
— the understanding of the similarities and differences in fine and applied art concepts.
— the nature of the questions and demands the fine artist asks of himself.
— fine art as an area of pure research and understanding to ensure continued personal growth.

### History of Art/Design/Architecture
Knowledge and ability to:
— recall and understand historical or current concepts, movements, philosophies, and works by individual and/or groups of artists, designers, architects.
— fine art as an area of pure research and understanding to ensure continued personal growth.

## SPECIALIZED DATA OF THE ARCHITECTURAL DESIGNER 4

Acquired, Stored, or Obtainable Data Related to:

### Problem Solving
Knowledge and ability to:
— think philosophically encompassing both rational and emotional aspects.
— generate, direct, and organize ideas and thoughts.
— acquire mental processes for facilitating imagination and logic.
— define and analyze problems relevant to need.
— ask and answer pertinent questions.
— order priorities.
— recall factual, emotional, and experiential data.
— intuit client and user needs and responses.
— acknowledge diverse value systems within the client/user context.
— make esthetic judgments and decisions based on user adaptability, activity, and function.
— verbalize clearly and succinctly any of the above (or more) when necessary.
— know difference between a solution and a concept.

### Process
Knowledge in and ability to effectively apply:
— design philosophy and principles (gestalt, line, space, shape, value, mass/void, contrast, repetition, time, change, motion, color, etc.) for specific uses in order to facilitate desirable user behavior.
— skills necessary in creating a built environment which successfully accommodates and promotes the changing needs and aspirations of its users.
— structural systems, engineering principles, mathematics, physics, drafting, construction methods, materials, and techniques.

### Tools/Materials
Skills and craftsmanship in:
— drawing, rendering, with graphite, pen and ink, felt tip, photography, papers, watercolor, matt boards, and drafting equipment.
— model building related to self-communication and presentation of information to clients.
— direct and mechanical transfer aids—Lucigraph, Art-O-Graph, Blueprints, Ozalids, printing processes, shading sheets, press-on letter forms, etc., as well as cameras, photo processing and projection equipment.
— basic carpentry and hand and power tools.

### Fine Art Studio
Knowledge and ability to use:
— various media processes in both two-dimensional and three-dimensional expressions.
— the understanding of the similarities and differences in fine and applied art concepts.
— the nature of the questions and demands the fine artist asks of himself.
— fine art as an area of pure research and understanding to ensure continued personal growth.

### History of Architecture/Design/Art
Knowledge and ability to:
— recall and understand historical or current concepts, movements, philosophies, and works by individual and/or groups of architects, designers, artists.
— recall and understand the cultural climates, value systems, and societies that produced any movement, concept, and work.

## COGNITION

The mental process by which we secure information, process, and apply it—the idea process—is called *cognition*. Formerly it was believed that this process was *linear* in nature. For example, language, the primary tool of communication, is linear, since it is composed of sounds uttered sequentially. Written language was probably developed to emulate the spoken word. Then words were formed into sentences, and eventually sentences were used to form paragraphs in a series of consecutive lines. Each sound, letter, word, sentence, paragraph must be executed and received in a linear progression in order to have its meaning grasped. However, even though data have been communicated in this fashion, once received in the brain, these data interrelate three-dimensionally in the cognitive process. It is as if billions of pieces of string, which represent data of various types were tied together in a single strand hundreds of thousands of miles long. When this single string is wound into a ball and compressed to the size of a large grapefruit, it could represent the brain, in which all pieces become related in a common mass by touching—literally, by becoming a part of one another.

Cognition and the interrelationships of the elements of which it is composed are outlined in Figures 1 to 4. (These divisions and classifications of information are not intended to be a complete explanation of the scientific complexities involved in the working of the brain. Rather, they have been condensed into a basic form to aid in the understanding of the thinking process. Figure 5 is a representation of that process in simplified form.) In Figures 1 to 4, notice that certain subjects are listed in multiple categories. Language, for instance, can be categorized in more than one data bank. When it is concerned with syntax (the way in which words are put together to form phrases, clauses, or sentences), language is factual. It can also be classified under experiential data, since it is an acquired skill that a child begins learning spontaneously through experience. This will hold true for countless other subjects as well.

5

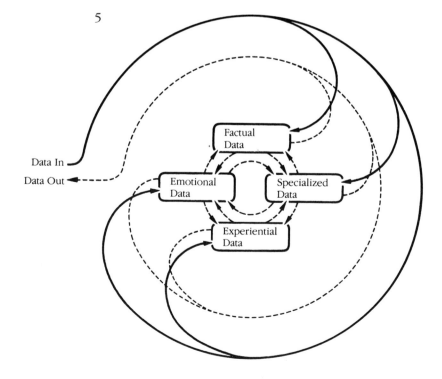

## VERBAL/IDEA EXPLORATION SYSTEMS

Since all forms of communication are preceded by a thought process, it is helpful for us to clarify and have a complete understanding of our own thinking before attempting to communicate ideas to others. One way to clarify thinking is to verbalize our thoughts, in written or in spoken form.

Although an artist will ultimately arrive at a visual expression, it is also true that the expression can only be as effective as the quality and clarity of the thinking and verbal exploration which preceded it. As a result, the ability to verbalize clearly to oneself and to others can make one a more effective artist.

### Brainstorming

Brainstorming is a simple and straightforward verbal exploration system that can produce dramatic results. It consists of the written recording of verbalized ideas generated through free association by a group gathered to consider a particular subject or problem. The most important advantage of brainstorming is the generation of ideas from multiple sources as a result of group participation. Because of this multiple involvement, there is a chance to hear ideas from different points of view. A situation is created where each new idea flows directly from one previously verbalized.

The physical mechanics of brainstorming are fairly simple. The psychological factors involved, however, are more difficult, since a large group of people must not only participate but cooperate as a unit to make the process productive. This can be managed effectively if guidelines for both the physical procedure and group behavior are established.

The procedure requires that there be a group of not less than three and not more than twenty-five participants, with an optimum number being between twelve and eighteen. One member of the group is designated to record ideas as they are generated. Everyone in the group must be able to refer to these ideas throughout the session, so they should be written legibly on a chalkboard or with a felt tip marker on large sheets of paper taped to a wall.

The guidelines of group behavior that need to be established and followed are extremely important. They are designed to create a relaxed atmosphere conducive to generating ideas. There should be no laughter or editorial comment, either positive or negative, when an idea is verbalized, so that no one in the group will hold back for fear of being ridiculed or intimidated. Everyone must be encouraged to relax and say whatever comes to mind. No one should be afraid to verbalize ideas, nor should they withhold them regardless of how strange or far removed they may sound.

It is very important to keep the procedures of brainstorming informal. Even when ideas are being generated so rapidly that everyone is speaking at once, the person recording them should make every effort to write everything down. Formal behavior, such as raising hands to speak, would defeat the purpose of brainstorming. It is distracting and does not allow for multiple free association—the reason for brainstorming in the first place.

Since brainstorming is an idea-generating process based on free association and uncensored input from several sources, many of the ideas generated may not be relevant to each person trying to formulate a solution to a problem. Therefore, immediately following the session, each individual may find it helpful to edit the master list and make a new list of those ideas that seem personally relevant to solving the project at hand. In this way, it is possible to formulate ideas that can be communicated visually.

For example, if we were given the simple exercise of visually communicating the concept "designate" by using words, pictures, or objects except the word "designate," after brainstorming the master list (Figure 6) could be edited. The new personal list could be then further clarified by dividing it into two categories. One category would be composed of ideas that seemed to relate more to the *forms* that an idea might take. The second category would incorporate those ideas that seemed to relate more to the *content* of a particular idea soution. It is possible that some of these ideas may overlap and appear in both categories. Examples of these two categorical lists—form and content—are given in Figures 7 and 8. Upon completing the form and content lists, still shorter, more specific lists can be assembled to group ideas that seem closely related. Completion of these lists of related ideas may reveal solution directions to the visual communication of "designate" (Figures 9, 10, 11). Through the use of brainstorming, an artist can solve actual problems as simply as this exercise was solved.

## RESULTS OF BRAINSTORMING—ONE HOUR WITH 25 PEOPLE

### DESIGNATE  6

| | | |
|---|---|---|
| measure | enclose | is real |
| degree | numb | sort out |
| decision | arrow | delete |
| release | divide | useful |
| mark | in common | detail |
| typical | dissect | stipulate |
| bulletin | penetrate | proofread |
| report | death | book |
| form | earth | slogan |
| telegram | life | spot |
| shout | stand out | code |
| testify | note | plaque |
| program | glove | flash cards |
| notify | date | promote |
| dictate | shock | cancel |
| forbid | S.O.S. | pick out |
| brainwash | road | customs |
| force | stop light | signature |
| truth | flag | lazy |
| stipulate | beacon | later |
| misjudge | symbols | export |
| marker | group | calligraphy |
| the best | member | objective |
| stimulate | compartment | accommodation |
| flag | individual | remove |
| brag | different | ordeal |
| show off | rare | declare |
| examine | gifted | characterize |
| example | valuable | professional |
| focus | reward | amateur |
| replace | erase | tape off |
| provoke | elite | recognize |
| organize | raise | class |
| expel | decision | familiar |
| reveal | cut off | sought after |
| direction | set out | design |
| decode | F-stop | put together |
| move | destruct | intent |
| diagram | opaque | unique |
| clarify | step forward | pronounce |
| lead | transparent | exaggerate |
| north | plastic | intense |
| diminish | fake | excite |
| south | simple | big deal |
| compass | pride | step-by-step |
| eliminate | educate | assemble |
| notice | assign | authority |
| illegal | Chinese | power |
| mistake | loud | tragedy |
| change | silence | comedy |
| progress | explode | theater |
| growth | surround | different |
| desire | enclose | the same |
| develop | kill | make noticeable |
| anoint | manipulate | place |
| claim | show | repeat |
| remember | refer | force |
| merit | reject | people |
| most important | encompass | crowd |
| bureaucracy | vanish | unusual |
| outstanding | center | object |
| index | reveal | segment |
| footnote | banish | freak |
| the one | undress | black market |
| **parenthesis** | enlighten | aside |
| equation | dress up | apart |
| set off | expose | educate |
| solution | gather | institutionalize |
| formula | portrait | bonus |
| recipe | borrow | name |
| compound | specialize | crowded |
| zenith | artist | ribbon |
| extract | make special | medallion |
| explain | special | charm |
| medium | law | specialize |
| outline | menu | seal |
| buoy | make known | decorate |
| stereotype | awareness | impose |
| clarify | which one | forget |
| standard | package | dinosaur |
| exposé | bag | prehistoric |
| cliché | sack | divide |
| atypical | box | split |
| cult | trunk | element |
| scrutinize | cover | atom |
| make obvious | enclose | physics |
| set apart | stamp | tell |
| open up | under | underline |
| exert | isolate | know |
| hold up | clothe | substantiate |
| identify | pronounce | isolate |
| expound | strip | outline |
| magnetize | discriminate | split |
| simplify | wrap | larger size |
| magnify | assign | edit |
| call attention | red tape | slash |
| click | government | rule |
| line up | subtraction | profound |
| check | relegate | specialize |
| explain | inform | reform |
| reveal | detail | tell how |
| underground | one-of-a-kind | instruct |
| clammy | study | explore |

## DESIGNATE (Cont)   6

punctuate
quote
surprise
explanatory
question
exclamation
answer
bibliography
glossary
pike
type
separate
position
schedule
complex
essential
distinct
divine
map
run down
precise
reminder
categorize
reveal
classify
precise
emphasis
odd
fine
discover
locate
unicorn
open
official
command
diagnosis
write
apart
qualify
import
depart
raise
test
job
announce
mix
ultimate
superficial
tag
italicize
trademark
time
label
chart
graph
arrange
explore
diagram
demarcation
gravestone
**neon sign**
monument
signal
"x"
boldface
color
cull
informative
handwriting
flash
symmetrical
perfect
resolve
centralized
graphic
centered
aligned
grid
best one
circle
bright
immaculate
on top
approve
top
pinnacle
most perfect
accurate
quality
excellence
highlight
order
pass
combine
differentiate
accentuate
listing
conscience
invisible
reflection
elect
grab

younger
uncover
#1
mark through
capitalize
area
"A," "B," "C"
language
obsolete
vote
decide
required
win
perfection
success
crate
order
barrel
distinct
lucky
extinct
advertise
placement
individualize
features
start
character
remote
medal
compete
departmentalize
innovate
begin
end
one of the above
timed
end
assemble
determine
deform
noticeable
pick out

## FORM   7

mark
marker
set off
make obvious
set apart
simplify
magnify
check
reveal
impose
larger size
separate
"x"
mark through
make obvious
arrow
divide
dissect
stand out
note
group
individual
different
cut off
set out
edit
position
classify
boldface
individualize
obvious
destruct
surround
enclose
encompass
expose
gather
make known
bag
sack
box
crate
barrel
split
distinct
tag
color
departmentalize
italicize
trunk
stamp
isolate
wrap
assign
delete
detail
book
slogan
telegram
listing
underline
punctuate
reminder
label
cull
pick out
cancel
remove
tape off
different
noticeable
repeat
force
segment
seal
decorate
quote
categorize
arrange
circle

## CONTENT   8

bulletin
report
form
notify
dictate
forbid
force
stipulate
expel
reveal
notice
illegal
mistake
change
desire
remember
most important
bureaucracy
outstanding
index
footnote
the one
parenthesis
equation
solution
formula
recipe
compound
extract
explain
clarify
standard
identify
call attention
explain
reveal
death
stand out
note
road
flag
reward
educate
assign
kill
refer
reject
law
awareness
discriminate
government
relegate
inform
detail
sort out
delete
stipulate
code
customs
signature
export
declare
characterize
sought after
design
put together
unique
step-by-step
assemble
authority
power
force
people
unusual
segment
educate
institutionalize
name
analysis
tell
know
specialize
reform
reveal
classify
map
emphasis
discover
locate
official
command
qualify
import
depart
test
announce
chart
graph
informative
centralized
aligned
best one
approve

most perfect
accurate
excellence
highlight
order
pass
differentiate
area
obsolete
required
advertise
individualize
features
remote
departmentalize
assemble

9

**Content:**

Notice, notify, illegal, the one, identify, call attention, explain, reveal, death, reward, law, inform, sought after, authority, force, name, tell, locate, advertise, features

**Form:**

Make obvious, set apart, reveal, separate, stand-out, individual, different, surround, expose, gather, make known, circle, boldface, marker

**One possible solution derived from above ideas:**

"Wanted" and "Reward" poster for a dangerous criminal with name set in boldface type and possibly circled with a marker

10

**Content:**

Government, bureaucracy, official, departmentalize, notify, dictate, forbid, stipulate, most important, index, identify, call attention, stand-out, inform, code, declare, unique, authority, power, force, unusual, segment, classify, emphasis, command, order

**Form:**

Mark, set off, make obvious, set apart, simplify, magnify, impose, larger size, separate, stand out, individualize, obvious, make known, color, stamp, assign, label, noticeable, categorize, underline

**One possible solution derived from above ideas:**

File folder or official government document stamped with large red letters: "Top Secret" or "Most Secret"

11

**Content:**

Import, export, customs, declare, approved, notify, stipulate, sort out, inform, refer, assign, identify, authority, tell, differentiate, pass, approve, official, locate

**Form:**

Mark, check, individual, classify, boldface, obvious, make known, bag, sack, box, crate, barrel, distinct, tag, trunk, stamp, wrap, assign, underline, label, noticeable, circle

**One possible solution derived from above ideas:**

A crate, barrel, or box stamped or marked "Approved for Export by Customs Authorities"

## Listing

Another method of verbal exploration that can be used to acquire ideas is a direct listing system. This method is similar to brainstorming, since it is accomplished by the uncensored free association of ideas related to a particular subject or problem. The major difference between brainstorming and listing is that the ideas in brainstorming come from multiple sources and the ideas in listing come from a single source.

This method is executed by simply starting at the top of the page and making a list of everything that relates to a particular subject. This system is quite common and usually functions adequately. Lists can also be very useful in reviewing, organizing, and isolating ideas that have been generated by other methods like brainstorming, or the next one to be discussed—verbal diagramming.

## Verbal Diagramming

For any creative thought system to be effective, it helps if it is as spontaneous as possible, with a minimum of restrictions—"shoulds," inhibitions, formal approaches—while maximizing thought processes in an almost free-association manner. Ideally, a method that allows the rapid results of thinking to be visually and effortlessly recorded is necessary so that the procedure of recording interferes as little as possible with the flow of thoughts. The following is suggested as one of the best systems used for encouraging creative thought exploration. The basic concept and application of this system is based on Tony Buzan's research and writing concerning the complexities and total use of the brain.*

The system suggested is that of an "accessible" diagrammatic approach. (By "accessible" we mean an open system, as opposed to a closed system that does not allow a free flow of thought.) Since organization in a linear language context can slow down and limit the possibilities of verbally exploring concepts, a diagrammatic approach that is not linear can help accelerate and expand verbal concept exploration. That is, if the elements of the diagram at no time form a completed circle, we are always free to insert data when and where it occurs in relation to appropriate areas in the diagram. Examples of accessible diagrams may be seen in Figures 12 and 13. This system is continually able to receive new or additional information. In linear organization, this option is almost impossible without some kind of reorganization being done first. Ostensibly, the accessible diagrammatic system allows one to be as candid, direct, and free as possible.

*Tony Buzan, *Use Both Sides of Your Brain* (New York: Dutton, 1976).

In order for this technique to become comfortable and worthwhile, at first it must be practiced frequently. Once the system becomes familiar, a significant improvement in identifying, acquiring, and organizing verbal concepts will be noted and appreciated.

The primary difference between this method and the vertical, linear method is that instead of starting from the top and working down, it starts with a key concept (word or phrase) and branches out as other ideas related to the concept occur. The advantages of working this way are numerous; they all help the brain to function more naturally and fully.

1. A primary or main idea is defined or stated, thus becoming an aid to more clearly defining the problem.

2. This type of diagrammatic structure allows for easier and faster addition of new information.

3. It becomes very easy to see links and connections among key concepts because of their proximity.

4. It is possible visually to interrelate data through the use of quickly drawn graphic devices such as arrows, ovals, and boxes.

5. When used for creative thinking, the open-ended nature of the diagram enables the brain to make new connections far more readily than the linear or list methods.

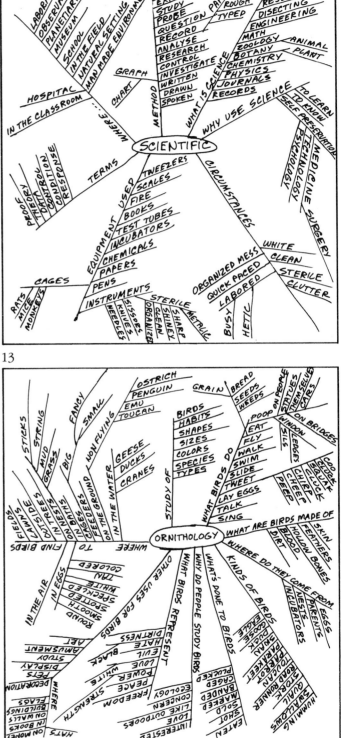

This system may appear messy and cluttered in comparison to the vertical, linear method. As a result of its spontaneous nature, it is; but this is necessary because spontaneity is one of the reasons it works so well. The following guidelines are helpful in using the system properly:

1. All words are printed; this is a quick form of recording and will make the diagram easier to read later.

2. All the words are printed on lines and all lines are connected to other lines.

3. The mind is kept as "free" as possible when diagramming. Any thinking about where things should go or whether to include them will slow down the process and reduce the number of ideas produced.

4. When using this method, the principle is to recall anything and everything that pertains to the central concept. Since the mind will generate ideas faster than they can be printed, there will be almost no pause in the process.

5. Do not worry about organization. Most of the time this will take care of itself. If it does not, reorganization can be done later when the preliminary diagram has been completed.*

6. Once the key concept or topic has been determined, the flow of thought related to that concept may be initiated by asking the questions why, when, how, who, where, what, etc. By initially asking and answering each of these questions in turn, particularly "why," there will be more than enough information to begin the diagramming process. Continuation of the diagram is then easily evolved by asking and aswering the same questions again or any others that may come to mind.

In the example diagrams (Figures 12, 13, 14), a number of ideas were generated very rapidly. Two of the examples (Figures 12 and 13) took less than twenty minutes each. The third (Figure 14) took an hour. All three examples could be reorganized if necessary; however, they are perfectly usable in their present form.

*Tony Buzan, *Use Both Sides of Your Brain,* (New York: Dutton, 1976) pp. 89–90.

14

### Organizing Logical Thought Processes

After a verbal exploration system has been completed and key concepts thoroughly explored, it may be beneficial to visually reorganize. This will ensure that the idea will still be clear even if time passes before it is again used for reference. Visual organization is equally helpful in clarifying and ordering thoughts in relation to the main idea. And even though visual organization is not the primary function of a diagrammatic system, in many cases it is a real help. Visual reorganization may also be necessary when a verbal or written presentation of an individual's thinking is required. An illustration of how one of the verbal diagrammatic systems has been reorganized may be seen in Figure 15.

Two widely accepted methods are used for visual organization: *lists* and *flow charts*. A list may be thought of as a traditional outline of acquired and recorded information. If a diagram is being used as an idea reference for the list, the main ideas are easily found in the diagram as a result of the graphic devices that have been used. These graphically emphasized ideas in turn become major headings on the list. Those thoughts placed in proximity to the main ideas on the diagram will become subheadings on the list in order of importance. Those ideas found to be extraneous can be eliminated.

Although a list is usually linear and vertical in nature, this is not necessarily always the case. Lists may also be executed in a horizontal manner; two or more may be developed on a page side by side so that they form columns of information. This approach gives the lists more flexibility in terms of the horizontal, as well as vertical, interrelationship of ideas.

A second method of visual organization is the flow chart. It is an easily understood and widely used approach to the visual organization of verbal material. Flow charts are often used because the charts—if well designed—are legible, easy to read, and afford an organization of material that can be clearly understood. This is made possible by the combination of verbal material with visual graphic devices that organize and direct the reader in an ordered step-by-step sequence.

In the use of both lists and flow charts, every effort should be exerted to make them as well organized and as logical as possible.

### VISUAL EXPLORATION OF IDEAS

When it becomes apparent that no further progress can be made in acquiring and developing an idea verbally, visual explorations related to that idea are usually begun. Visual exploration is that process whereby an idea takes tangible, visible form. For example, no matter how thoroughly a particular color has been verbally described, it cannot be completely visualized and understood until it has been seen in physical reality. In the same way, an idea that is intended eventually to take visual form cannot be completely understood, or its quality completely evaluated, until it is actually seen.

Every idea can be expressed through numerous methods and media—the components of process. Each idea can be executed in any number of visual combinations of these process elements. When considered in this way, it becomes apparent that the visual possibilities for a single idea and the exploration of such possibilities are limitless; and that ultimately these explorations and considerations can only be accomplished visually. Therefore, it is imperative to realize that *visual decisions must be made visually*.

The most direct method of visual exploration is a deliberate step-by-step modification of an existing image (Figure 16). This type of visual variation can be accomplished both two- and three-dimensionally with numerous combinations of methods and media. Throughout history, many of the world's greatest artists used this step-by-step method with repeated success. For example, visual variation was a favorite technique of Paul Klee (Figure 17), and many of his works could not have been produced without its use. Beginning artists will discover how useful the method is for making visual decisions as soon as they learn to adapt it to different methods and media.

15

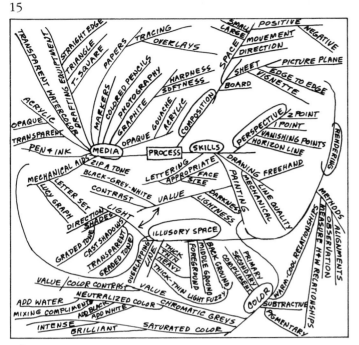

PROCESS SKILLS IN:

| ILLUSORY SPACE | MEDIA | COMPOSITION | COLOR |
|---|---|---|---|
| PERSPECTIVE | DRAFTING | SPACE | ADDITIVE/LIGHT |
| HORIZON LINE | EQUIPMENT | RELATIONSHIPS | SUBTRACTIVE/PIGM. |
| VANISHING POINT | STRAIGHT EDGE | POSITIVE-NEGATIVE | VALUE |
| 1 POINT PERSPECTIVE | T-SQUARE | SCALE | V./COLOR CONTRASTS |
| 2 POINT PERSPECTIVE | TRIANGLE | LARGE-SMALL | PRIMARY |
| DRAWING | PAINT | SHEET/BOARD | SECONDARY |
| FREEHAND/MECHAN. | TRANS. WATERCOLOR | PICTURE PLANE | COMPLIMENTS |
| LINE QUALITY | GOUACHE | EDGE-TO-EDGE | SATURATED |
| HEAVY/BOLD | ACRYLIC | VIGNETTE | INTENSE/BRILLIANT |
| THICK/THIN | OPAQUE TRANS. | DIRECTION | CHROMATIC GREYS |
| LIGHT | PEN AND INK | MOVEMENT | NEUTRALIZED COLOR |
| FUZZY | MARKERS | | ADD WATER |
| LETTERING | COLORED PENCILS | | ADD BLACK |
| OVERLAPPING- | GRAPHITE PENCILS | | ADD WHITE |
| PLANES-OBJECTS | HARD-SOFT | | MIX COMPLIMENTS |
| FOREGROUND | PAPERS | | WARM-COOL |
| MIDDLEGROUND | TRACING PAPER | | COLOR RELATIONSHIPS |
| BACKGROUND | OVERLAYS | | |
| RENDERING | MECHANICAL AIDS | | |
| VALUE | LETTERSET | | |
| LIGHT/DARK | ZIP-A-TONE | | |
| CONTRAST | LUCYGRAPH | | |
| BLACK-GREY-WHITE | PHOTOGRAPHY | | |
| LIGHT | | | |
| DIRECTION | | | |
| SHADE | | | |
| GRADED TONE | | | |
| CAST SHADOWS | | | |
| REFLECTED LIGHT | | | |

16

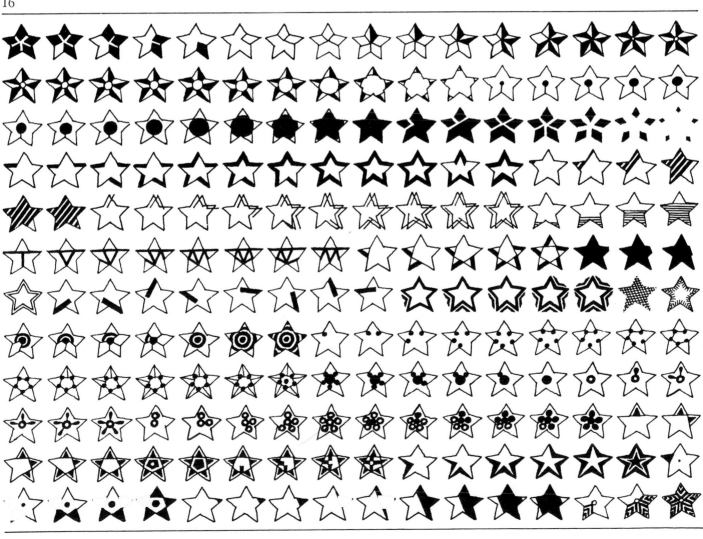

Among the various methods of visual exploration, two of the most important are roughs and the process of working with transparent and opaque overlays. Both are widely used in various forms of visual art. When used appropriately, they are effective methods for experimenting with various combinations.

Visual *roughs* are adaptable to all forms of visual art in either two or three dimensions. The most common and useful is the daily working rough. This type of rough is created for the sole purpose of visual exploration. Occasionally, artists forget that the primary purpose of a rough is simply that—a flexible, visual exploration—not a finished, committed visual expression. To forget the purpose of a rough can result in limited creativity as well as wasted time.

17

Paul Klee, *Assyrian Game,* 1923 © 1981, Copyright by COSMOPRESS, Geneva & ADAGP, Paris

The process of working with *overlays* is another indispensable method of visual exploration. Overlays can be transparent or opaque, and each has its own particular function and advantage.

Transparent overlays can be made from any form of transparent material. The most commonly used materials are tracing paper and acetate, and the use of each is dependent on the need of the artist. For example, tracing paper would be appropriate for dry media and acetate for wet. These transparent sheets can be placed over a previously executed image so that corrections and changes can be made without redrawing the entire image. Working with transparent overlays in this way dramatically reduces the time required to visualize multiple solutions to any given problem.

Opaque overlays are used to achieve very similar results. This technique is a direct method for making multiple visual variations and is adaptable to almost any situation, both two- and three-dimensional. For example, opaque overlays can be very useful in quickly visualizing a color change in a specific area of an image. In this particular situation, an opaque color swatch is painted, or a color paper selected and cut to the desired size and shape; then it is placed over the area in question to experiment with a visual possibility. In like manner, opaque overlays can be adapted to countless other explorations of visual variations.

The idea process is systematic and basic. Also, the entire procedure of acquiring, researching, generating, identifying, analyzing, defining, formulating, selecting, developing, and refining ideas can be a most exciting, stimulating aspect of creating art. And, with a solid idea foundation, communicative expressions of art that possess conceptual strength and integrity can be created.

# SECTION TWO

# 12

CONTENT

## CONTENT—IDEA AND COMMUNICATION COMBINED

For a creative expression to possess meaning or significance, first it must incorporate an idea. Second, if the idea is to have meaning or significance to others than the artist, it must be communicated through a process. It is the meaning or significance contained within any visual expression that is called *content*. Therefore, content is the result of combining idea and communication.

We can divide content into two separate categories: unintentional and intentional. The first of these two—unintentional content—can occur in a variety of ways found in forms resulting from natural visual phenomena (Figures 1 and 2). In these instances, content is supplied as a result of an individual's personal observation, experience, and imagination. In a similar way, unintentional content can be found in the work of craftspersons, architects, and product designers—those who may consider themselves concerned only with fulfilling a functional need. In many cases, however, these works may be perceived as communicating a particular idea, even though this may not have been intended.

The second category—intentional content—is the result of an earnest desire to communicate a specific idea through a visual or visual-verbal expression. This type of content is our major concern and is the basis of the rest of this chapter.

## TYPES OF INTENTIONAL CONTENT

In Chapter 10, we discussed the types of communication that can occur among human beings—intellectual, emotional, and a combination of both. Identical categories were also presented in Chapter 11. Logically, then, since content is the meaning or significance imparted by a work through some combination of *communication* and *idea,* it is possible for us to discuss content as being emotional, intellectual, and a combination of both.

In actuality, intellectual and emotional content usually exist simultaneously. However, for purposes of discussion and evaluation, we will treat them independently.

## EMOTIONAL CONTENT

We can describe the emotional response evoked by a work of art as a "feeling" response. This feeling response is caused by the emotional content that has been incorporated in the artist's work. We can define emotional content in art, then, as the communication of an idea expressed visually as a feeling.

As individuals, all of us are uniquely different from one another; but we all share many common characteristics. One of these shared traits is our ability to feel and respond to emotional stimulus; again, though, the way in which each person feels and responds is uniquely individual. This kind of variation in emotional response to a given situation can be illustrated by observing three individual, initial responses to a confrontation with a spider. One person may show little or no interest. A second person may be repulsed or terrified, while a third might be fascinated and totally unafraid. The second and third of these three individual responses are emotionally strong and specific; however, they are the result of completely different emotions—fear and fascination.

Just as people react in different ways emotionally to all kinds of information, they respond in different ways emotionally to art information. Therefore, having insight into human emotional responses evoked by given stimuli can be invaluable to us as artists when we wish to express ideas and feelings through emotional content. (See Figures 3–13 for emotional content examples.)

### Why It Is Used

Even though individuals may differ in relation to culture, education, or experience, basic emotions are universally shared. Also, while it may be possible for someone consciously to avoid the acquisition of an intellectual education, it is virtually impossible to avoid an emotional education. Therefore, since emotion is an intrinsic part of everyone's individual character, emotional content can be thought of as having the capability of being widely recognized and understood.

Because of its almost limitless flexibility, emotional content has powerful communication qualities. With it we are able to obtain a desired, specific response, such as excitement, fear, anger, sorrow, happiness, melancholy. Or, we can evoke a less specific, less direct response of a more subtle nature by shading or combining emotions in various degrees.

Since success in communicating an idea can be measured according to the strength of the response and emotional content can be an excellent vehicle for eliciting a response, we can consider emotional content a very effective communication tool.

## Who Uses It

Emotional content is extensively and effectively used in all forms of art. Fashion designers, industrial designers, architectural designers and interior designers, as well as most studio artists and craftspersons, depend on emotional content to elicit responses. In the visual expressions of each of these disciplines, marvelous communications exist as a result of the emotional content imparted to them. For instance, package designers use emotional content for the major portions of their visual communications, and millions of people buy packaged products based on that content. In the same way, many graphic designers use emotional content frequently and effectively to accomplish a wide range of communication goals for a mass audience—television and magazine advertisements, billboards, posters, and so on.

In the visual arts, emotional content is by far the most prevalent type used. This is particularly true since emotional content is the only type recognized by an undifferentiated audience. For example, a work of fine art can be compared to a symphony. In relation to music, most people are unaware of such specialized components as theory, structure, and orchestration, so they cannot respond to any content other than emotional. In the studio arts, this is no less true. Few people other than artists have the specialized knowledge to recognize any other type of content.

1

Photographer, Marty Robins

2

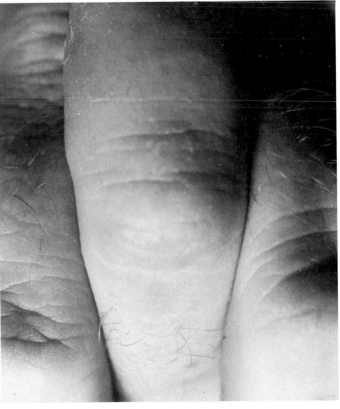

Photographer, Marty Robins

## Ways It Can Be Used

Anyone can use emotional content to accomplish a given responsive goal. For example, politicians and governments often use it as a manipulative tool known as propaganda. During World War II, many films were released for mass audience consumption in which the enemy was portrayed as having few, if any, redeeming characteristics. "Our boys" were portrayed as smart, humorous, courageous, honest, humane, and frequently handsome. On the other hand, the enemy was stupid, cowardly, dull, devious, cruel, and more often than not, ugly. These propaganda vehicles were calculated by the government and the motion picture industry to elicit a desired emotional response from the viewer and, during their day, they were very successful.

Another example of the use of emotional content can be seen in the field of fashion design. Clothing, in its most fundamental aspect, acts primarily to cover and protect the human body. However, with the addition of nonfunctional features such as color, patterns, prints, styling, and textures like lace, silk, satin, fur, and so on, clothing becomes dramatically imbued with emotional content. In this way, clothing not only satisfies the basic need for protection and warmth, it also satisfies a deep emotional need to appear and feel attractive.

These are just two of the many ways in which emotional content can be used.

3. The imagery in this sculpture suggests an entity containing multiple apertures, one of which has metallic, barracuda-like teeth. Consequently, the work has a powerful, threatening quality that evokes an emotional response of apprehension and terror.

4. Precise, delicate shapes as well as purity of form, give this ancient jar a sense of grace, elegance and strength. Such qualities elicit emotional responses of security and tranquility.

5. This painting combines a rich mixture of spontaneously executed curvilinear, organic, and accidental shapes. In this way, it emotionally communicates a warm and charming romanticism.

3

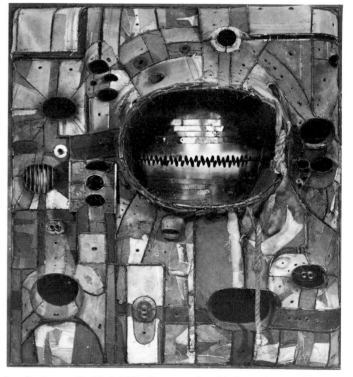

Lee Bontecou, *Untitled,* 1961. Canvas and welded metal, 72 x 66¼ x 26". Collection of Whitney Museum of American Art

## Methods Of Gaining Insight Into Emotions

While acquiring a working knowledge of the technical skills needed to bring idea and communication to visual realization, we can also concentrate on methods that will help us incorporate desired content in our work. In the case of emotional content, there are many ways of doing this.

Since emotions themselves are universal—that is, happiness is happiness regardless of the context—it is realistic to assume that a good place to begin a study of emotions is with our own. Honest self-examination is a direct method that can result in the revelation and clarification of feelings—likes, dislikes, beliefs, habits, prejudices—as well as the reasons for those feelings.

One way to aid in the process of self-examination is to keep a written record of thoughts and feelings as they occur. It is not necessary that this information be intended for public consumption; in fact, it would be better if it were kept private so that it can be as candid and free as possible. Keeping a record is an excellent method, since it provides a convenient reference to past thoughts and feelings. Trying to recall these thoughts and emotions without any recorded source of reference is difficult and can diminish potential insight—one of the goals of self-examination.

4

Earthenware Funerary Jar, Late Neolithic period, about 2000 B.C. Courtesy Haags Gemeentemuseum, The Hague

5

Henri Matisse, *Helene with Blue Jewel*, 1937.
(c)S.P.A.D.E.M., Paris/V.A.G.A., New York, 1981

Gaining an insight into our own thoughts and emotions in turn assists us in gaining insight into those of others. Self-examination is one method for doing this; another way is through group discussion. Group discussions are beneficial because we can get a fresh point of view in relation not only to our own thoughts and feelings, but to those of others as well. To increase the effectiveness of group discussions, several things can be done. For instance, before gathering a group for discussion, it can be helpful to determine a topic of mutual interest. Then, if those participating are informed in advance of the topic, they will have an opportunity to do some preliminary thinking. Finally, if the members of the group know they are not required to reveal "deep, dark secrets," they will feel more comfortable, relaxed, and eager to participate. Following these simple steps will result in a successful and effective exchange of thoughts and feelings.

Insight into the thoughts and feelings of others can also be obtained through simple observation. Understanding what the needs and circumstances of people are for any given situation can assist in the understanding of their behavior and responses. For example, the reasons people go to a bar are different from those for going to a place of worship, or a theater or a shopping mall, even though all of these are basically places where people assemble. So observation of situations

6. The wide open, laughing mouth and the smiling eyes of this dance mask from Ceylon communicate a mood of hilarity and excitement. Such a mood stimulates the pleasurable emotion of joy.

7. In this painting, simplicity of shape, contrast of scale, and contrast of value are combined with immediacy of execution to express the artist's melancholy feelings about social oppression and civil war.

8. In this Barcelona apartment house, sensually fluid, organic forms and spaces evoke feelings of warmth, ease, and security. In this way, the architect has been responsive to the basic emotional needs of the inhabitants.

9. The emotional content associated with whimsy and childhood can be felt when viewing these delicate, linear elements and slightly irregular, simple forms.

10. Cannibalism and cruelty are clearly and directly communicated in this 19th century painting; the feelings evoked are undeniably those of repulsion and horror.

6

*King Coconut,* Ceylon. Collection Pearl Binder,
The Hamlyn Group Picture Library

Robert Motherwell, *Elegy to the Spanish Republic, No. 45,* 1960.
Collection, the artist

Casa Mila by Antoni Gaudi, Photograph courtesy Division of
Architecture, Texas Tech University

Oliver Andrews, *Spring Song:* from *Metal Sculpture* by John Lynch,
(c)1957 The Viking Press, Inc., and Viking Penguin, Inc. (Alan Gallery)

Francisco Goya, *Saturn Devouring His Children,* 1818.
The Prado, Madrid

like these will provide information about people, their thoughts and their emotions. Again, it can be helpful if these observations related to time, place, numbers, reasons, and so on are recorded; this information then will be readily accessible when needed.

Even though emotions are universally standard, it is necessary for us to be aware that the stimulus needed to evoke a certain feeling response can vary according to cultural conditioning. Stimulus in relation to cultural context, then, is a variable that we must consider. For example, in many Western countries black is the symbol of death and evokes a response of seriousness and austerity in relation to that event. However, in Japan these same emotions are evoked by the color white because white, rather than black, is the Japanese symbol of death. Obviously, then, due to different attitudes, similar emotions can be activated by different colors, or a variety of other variables.

The evolution of the automobile in two separate cultures illustrates how varying emotional responses to the same stimulus can occur. While the functional purpose of the automobile is unmistakably transportation, the emotional content that determines the style of the car may differ from culture to culture. An illustration can be found in a comparison between automobiles designed for the United States and those designed for Western Europe during the 1950s. In the United States, the automobile had become more than a vehicle for transportation; it had assumed the position of a status symbol. Size; speed; ornamentation; color; comforts such

11

Edward Hopper, *Early Sunday Morning,* 1930, oil on canvas, 35 x 60". Collection of Whitney Museum of American Art

11. In this painting, the artist has combined a succinct, elegant idea with simplicity of composition and repetition of size, shape, and position to create a moment and mood rich with subtleties. Almost at once we can feel a certain quietude, serenity, and peace as well as a sense of loneliness, isolation, and despair.

12. The emotional content in this illustration re-creates pleasant associations with homegrown vegetables, cozy fragrances of a rustic kitchen, and the festivities of the harvest moon. All of these combine to communicate a nostalgic feeling of warmth and security.

as space, leather or velour upholstery, power steering and electric windows; all were important not as a result of their function, but because of emotional requirements of self-esteem, success, and so on. In comparison, in Western Europe the automobile had been seen quite clearly as functional, and the esthetic, including the style, was a direct result of that function. Therefore, an automotive designer would not have been addressing European cultural and emotional needs by designing a large, four-door, powerful sedan for mass production. Such an approach, at that time, was more correct and acceptable in the United States.

Conclusively, we propose that it is helpful for artists—even those who rely heavily on emotional intuition for their expressions—to acquire an insight into emotions and their stimuli in order to use emotional content successfully.

12

Package designed by Sue Crolick for Northrup King Co.

13

Notre Dame du Haut by Le Corbusier.
Photograph courtesy Division of Architecture, Texas Tech University

13. Curvilinear forms and sloping planes combined in a massive feeling structure communicate the emotional content we associate with places of worship—warmth, security, strength, and joy.

## INTELLECTUAL CONTENT

In comparison with emotional content, which concentrates on obtaining a feeling response, intellectual content attempts to stimulate an entirely different kind of response. The response can be described as intellectual comprehension resulting from a visual or visual-verbal communication of an idea. When considering intellectual content, then, we must realize that it can range from a single "Left Turn Only" sign to a detailed explanation of the theory of relativity. (See Figures 14–25 for intellectual content examples.)

### Basis Of Intellectual Content

To produce intellectual comprehension, it is necessary to base intellectual content on common knowledge previously acquired and retained by the desired audience. It is equally important to identify this common knowledge. It may be composed of an endless number of elements, such as customs, beliefs, desires, facts, figures, language, skills, education, experience. It is usually acquired during a lifetime of questioning, thinking, experiencing, conversing, reading, writing, researching—in essence, any process that systematically obtains and requires storage of information. Any combination or combinations of this kind of information as shared by a designated audience can be drawn upon by the artist as a resource for intellectual content.

Obviously, we do not all share the same common knowledge because of differences in culture, age, learning abilities, or countless other factors. For example, a seven-year-old child may understand the fundamentals of addition and subtraction when they are explained, but have absolutely no comprehension of the principles of calculus if they are presented. In a similar way, if French is used to explain the fundamentals of addition and subtraction to the same child when that child only speaks and understands English, there will be no comprehension of the attempted communication. These two examples illustrate why it is important for us to be aware of the audience's stored knowledge if we hope to obtain a response through the use of intellectual content.

14

Artist, Gahan Wilson. Reproduced by Special Permission of *Playboy* Magazine; Copyright ©, 1970 by Playboy

## Ways It Can Be Used

We can use intellectual content in numerous ways for a variety of reasons. Usually, it is most effective in situations where intellectual comprehension must be obtained quickly and precisely. For this reason, it is frequently used as a form of communication in visual art forms as well as in nonart forms such as language, chemistry, and math.

Symbols are one of the most common visual forms that incorporate intellectual content to stimulate an immediate response. Such symbols are representative of verbal explanations that have become so standardized that the visual alone communicates the verbal without its being stated. Chemical formulas and sign language are examples of such symbols, although both require a specialized audience to respond to the intellectual content. Examples of standardized visual symbols that communicate direct information quickly and precisely to a less specialized audience are a skull and crossbones indicating danger, the visual designation of men's and women's restrooms, and road signs and signals for motorists.

Visual symbols can also be combined with verbal explanations to clarify information. This is done to make intellectual comprehension as complete as possible. Some examples of visual-verbal expressions of intellectual content may be a picture accompanying a definition in the dictionary, diagrams with directions on a package, or graphs that illustrate statistical information.

Language is the most common example of a verbal form that uses intellectual content to achieve a response. Gestures may also accompany speech to emphasize or ensure intellectual understanding. Like visual symbols, many of these gestures—even without language—are able to communicate the same message as a direct verbal statement. A shrug of the shoulders to indicate "I don't know" is just one example of this kind of communication. Finally, visual narratives, such as cartoons, may be substituted for entire verbal explanations and still retain the same intellectual content in the communication (Figure 14).

These are just a few examples of many ways in which intellectual content can be used to achieve a response of intellectual comprehension.

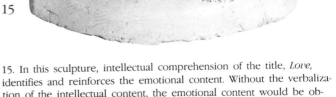

15

Marisol, *Love,* 1962, Plaster and glass (Coca Cola Bottle), 6 1/4 x 4 1/8 x 8 1/8".
Collection, the Museum of Modern Art, New York. Gift of Claire and Tom Wesselmann

15. In this sculpture, intellectual comprehension of the title, *Love,* identifies and reinforces the emotional content. Without the verbalization of the intellectual content, the emotional content would be obscure.

## Why It Is Used

Intellectual content can be instrumental in direct communication with oneself, other individuals, or large numbers of people. Any situation that demands direct, precise communication is appropriate for the use of intellectual content.

For example, intellectual content can be very effective in clarifying complicated information and the processes used to obtain it. Asking and answering questions, thinking, discovering, recalling, investigating, analyzing, and problem solving are all processes that require intellectual comprehension of information by a single individual or a large group. The use of intellectual content in these situations makes the communication of information easier and increases the chances of understanding.

Intellectual content is also useful in the personal communication processes of creating and satisfying individual curiosity. It stimulates the learning and self-improvement that result in personal, social, and economic advancement and contributions. Intellectual content is also necessary in the area of instruction. It is used in the classroom to teach fundamental facts and figures; and in the wider scope of living it is used to better inform society on changing issues, such as in science, government, and economics.

As these examples illustrate, it is the quality of directly informing an audience that makes intellectual content a frequent and widely used tool of communication.

## INTELLECTUAL CONTENT IN STUDIO AND APPLIED ART

Many contemporary studio artists communicate almost exclusively with emotional content. A powerful emotional response, rather than an intellectual understanding of specific information, is as much as many studio artists can hope—or even wish—to obtain from their audience.

One of the major reasons for this is that the very nature of studio art is not necessarily concerned with direct and specific communication. If it were, only a very small audience could be reached on an intellectual level, since this type of communication is dependent on shared common knowledge. The knowledge required would have to be very specialized, so it would probably be common to only a relatively small group composed completely of artists. Furthermore, in contemporary studio art, this small, specialized group can be reduced to an audience of one, because there are no existing consensual criteria among studio artists. More simply, this means that each individual artist makes decisions about good/bad, valid/invalid, correct/incorrect based on personal criteria. This makes the use of intellectual content very difficult in studio art.

There are situations, of course, where intellectual content can be utilized effectively in studio art. For example, an artist can entitle a work or body of work in such a way that a verbal, intellectual communication reinforces the visual communication. However, a lay audience cannot rely on these intellectual clues, because studio artists may use titles that bear no immediately apparent relationship to the image. Or they may use titles only as a tool for cataloguing their works.

We have suggested that many studio artists do not want to direct the response of their audience as specifically as they would with intellectual content. But this is one of the primary reasons that intellectual content is so important to the applied arts. In these disciplines, on most occasions, communication must be as clear and direct as possible, and it is essential that a designated audience, large or small, not only understand but respond to that communication. With intellectual content, we are able to direct the response of an audience by being aware of and utilizing common knowledge relevant to the communication.

16–17. Ken Dixon, *White Sand Shift,* 1980. Private Collection

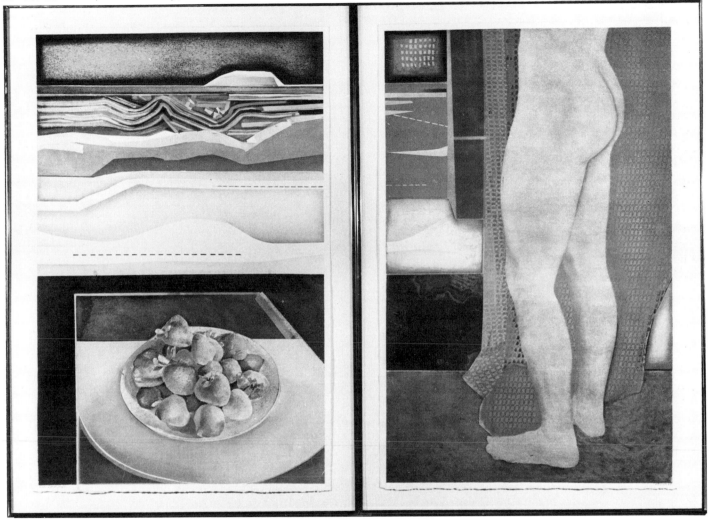

16,17. These two paintings are from a series entitled *White Sand Shift.* The title, in relation to the imagery, suggests that the artist was not primarily concerned—either visually or verbally—with direct and specific intellectual content.

18

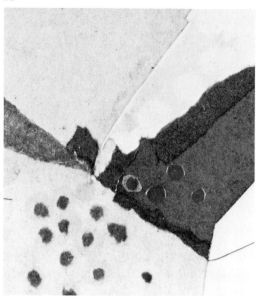

Tracy Hart, *Untitled*

18,19. Frequently, titles are used only for cataloging purposes, not for communication of any content. In both these examples, titles were felt to be unnecessary or harmful since a title could limit a viewer's perception and response. Therefore, the designation of *Untitled* was used.

19

Marty Robins, *Untitled,* 1981

20

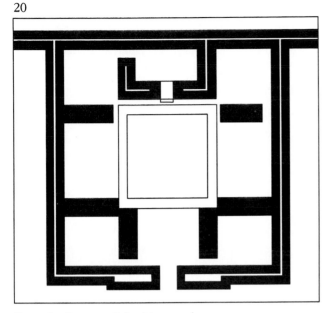

Floor plan for a pre-Columbian temple

20. Floor plans are excellent examples of visual communication containing intellectual content. This plan can be read as a large single unit (the entire temple), and as sub-units (the interior spaces) that are proportional to the larger whole.

21. Without the intellectual content of the title, the meaning of this sculpture would be uncertain. With the title, *Rain Ritual Fragment,* however, the meaning is more apparent. The suspended adobe forms can be seen as raindrops and the four horizontal projections near the top as the four directions of the compass. All these combine to suggest that the form could be used as a focal point in a ritual.

22. The visual similarities between the configurations of the human brain and a nuclear explosion can be intellectually comprehended in this graphic statement. By containing the image of an explosion within the silhouette of a head, a strong symbol has been created to reinforce the visual-verbal communication of the title.

21

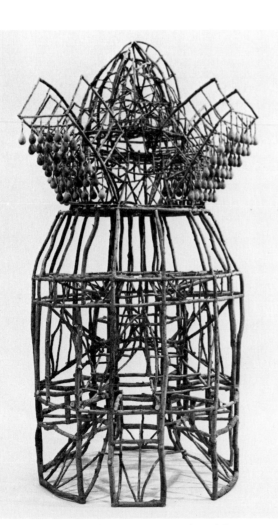

Frank Cheatham, *Rain Ritual Fragment,* 1981, 60 x 40".

22

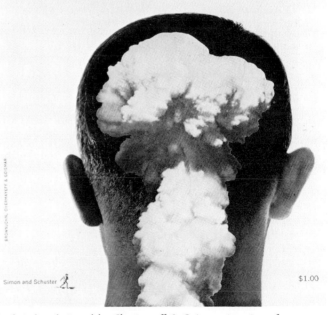

Book jacket designed by Chermayeff & Geismar Associates for *Common Sense and Nuclear Warfare,* 1960

23

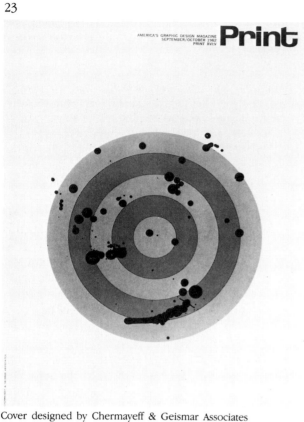

AMERICA'S GRAPHIC DESIGN MAGAZINE
SEPTEMBER/OCTOBER 1962
PRINT XVI:V **Print**

Cover designed by Chermayeff & Geismar Associates
for *Print* Magazine

24

Jerry Uelsmann, *1964.*

25

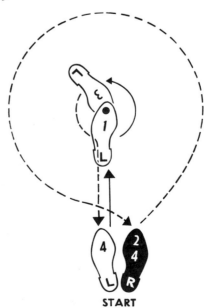

Andy Warhol, *Fox Trot,* 1961.
Photo courtesy of Leo Castelli Gallery, New York

23. This magazine cover is intended to communicate intellectually to a specific group—artists and designers involved in visual-verbal communication to mass audiences. The target is an intellectual communication of the marketing concept of "target groups"; and, the ink spots intellectually communicate an art process.

24. This photograph intellectually communicates information about trees that is not often perceived. That is, the entire shape of a tree is essentially the same as one of its smaller parts—the leaf. Additionally, the vein structure of the leaf is repetitive of other structures within the tree—the roots and the branches.

25. This simple, graphic painting has been specifically designed to be viewed on the floor in order to aid in the intellectual communication of an extremely complicated dance step.

26. The primary content in this work is intellectual. Once this content is comprehended, the emotional content is revealed and intense feelings of horror and fear are elicited. The war memorial of the soldiers raising the American flag at Iwo Jima is intellectually recognizable. However, in this situation it is out of the context of honor and glory. By placing the memorial in a hot dog stand and by adding to it a chalkboard tombstone with a counting device, the artist has presented war and death as being commonplace and flexible enough to fit any situation.

## COMBINED EMOTIONAL
## AND INTELLECTUAL CONTENT

Emotional and intellectual content are inseparable except for the purpose of discussion. Both are present in every form of communication, even if one or the other is completely unintentional or present to a very small degree. However, an optimum combination of emotional and intellectual content in art occurs when there is conscious control of the degree of each in the final communication. In these instances, emotional and intellectual content combine to reinforce one another and enhance the overall communication. Since a complete person is both emotional and rational, knowledgable usage of this combination can be an intriguing and satisfying form of communication.

An example of an intentional combination of emotional and intellectual content may be found in any individual's home. Ultimately, the home is a visual expression that communicates emotionally and intellectually both to oneself and to others. Initially, however, a house may be conceived as a functional shelter that incorporates certain systems which make it more livable. How large the house is, what materials will be used to construct it, where it will be located, decisions about heating, cooling, plumbing, storage, and ventilation are just a few of the many issues to be dealt with in planning the house. This realistic concern eventually manifests itself in the form of intellectual content; however, it is not the only concern.

The quality and configuration of the spaces, ornamentation, personal belongings, furnishings, color, texture, and so on are all largely based on emotional content as a result of emotional need. These qualities, however, do not exclude intellectual content in terms of discernible function.

The interior spaces of the home, and the objects found in it, reveal a great deal about the emotional and intellectual makeup of the occupants. This emotional and intellectual communication may range from warmth, comfort, relaxation, and individual integrity to aggression, tension, success, or social status. Eventually, these two components—intellectual and emotional—of an individual's home become so intertwined that they are ultimately dependent on one another.

The combination of intellectual and emotional content, when used correctly, is the most complete form of communication; used incorrectly, it can be the most misleading. To lovingly embrace someone and simultaneously shriek "I hate you!" results in a disturbingly contradictory message. Obviously, the emotional and intellectual content do not reinforce but deny one another, so that there is a conflict in the message and the response. A similar conflict would occur if a textbook for physics were to be typeset in an ornate formal script. Although the intellectual content of the information may be correct, the emotional content of the letter forms would seem inappropriate for the subject.

When the reinforcing and unifying factors inherent within emotional and intellectual content are recognized by the skilled artist, it is possible to utilize proper amounts of each to communicate an idea. (See Figures 26–39 for combined intellectual/emotional content examples.)

26

Edward Kienholz, *The Portable War Memorial,* 1968. Collection Museum Ludwig, Köln

## Why They Are Combined

It has been stated that emotional content is "the communication of an idea expressed visually or visually-verbally to obtain a feeling response"; and intellectual content has been defined as "intellectual comprehension resulting from a visual or visual-verbal communication of an idea through a process." Logically, the combination of these two forms of content in a single expression has the potential of eliciting simultaneously both a feeling response and intellectual comprehension. This serves not only to strengthen the communication, but greatly increases the chances of obtaining a response from a much broader, more diverse audience. Initially, those who may not completely understand the intellectual content may respond to the emotional content, or vice versa. When they respond to one or the other, the second form of content then becomes clearer and in turn reinforces the initial response to the communication. For example, the use of a skull and crossbones with the English word "poison" combines emotional and intellectual content that is capable of reaching a large audience which may not share exact intellectual data. Children or foreign-speaking adults may not respond to the word "poison," but the emotional content of the symbol of the skull and crossbones still communicates danger or warning.

By consciously adjusting the amounts of emotional or intellectual content, we can create multiple levels of and subtle variations in communication. The primary level of communication is made as direct as possible when emotional and intellectual content are combined in order to avoid misunderstanding or confusion. On secondary levels, many subtle forms of communication occur because every individual's emotional and intellectual data vary. For example, the scientific equation

27

Henri Rousseau, *The Dream,* 1910, oil on canvas, 6'8½" x 9'9½". Collection, The Museum of Modern Art, New York. Gift of Nelson A. Rockefeller

$E = MC^2$ is quickly comprehended by many people as the theory of relativity; this is the primary level of communication. On secondary levels, some people may know that this theory was formulated by Albert Einstein. Fewer may be able to define the terms in the equation. And a very small percentage, such as highly specialized scientists, may not only understand but be able to explain the intricacies of the theory. In the same way, secondary levels of communication in visual or visual-verbal expressions can create a richer, more interesting experience for the audience.

In addition to a richer expression, a timeless form of communication can be created by combining emotional and intellectual content. An example of this lasting quality may be found in many works that were created primarily for intellectual reasons, but that with the passage of time have acquired a stronger emphasis on emotional content. The works of primitive artists are classic examples of such timeless forms of expression. These artists created such items as cooking vessels, clothing, and religious articles for primarily intellectual, functional reasons. However, the personal emotions that were incorporated in these primitive articles have enabled them to communicate emotionally in an age where the intellectual content has become unimportant.

Similarly, in language certain phrases are coined initially for purposes of intellectual communication. However, after being used for a certain length of time, the emotional thrust of a particular culture, region, or people then becomes the primary content in the visual or visual-verbal expression. For example, the word "cuckoo" was originated to describe a bird of the family Cuculidae. However, over a period of time, the use and the meaning of the word has been altered. It

28

29

Pre-Columbian flat clay stamp. Private Collection

Head fragment from Vera Cruz, pre-Columbian. Private Collection.

27. When this painting is considered with its title, *The Dream,* both the primary and secondary levels of content can be easily seen. The primary intellectual content of the title stimulates secondary emotional feelings about a utopian fantasy that is abundant with rich and sensual delights.

28,29. The flat clay stamp on the left was originally intended for imprinting. The head fragment on the right was, perhaps, for religious activities. In both cases, however, the intellectual content is no longer relevant so it is the emotional that has emerged as the primary content. For instance, the richly decorated surface of the stamp immediately invites a tactile response while visually evoking feelings of charm and delight. Similarly, the purity and symmetry of the head contains a remote quality that suggests an austere serenity.

is now primarily used to communicate a description of an idiot or a fool rather than a bird. This meaning has evolved as a result of significant emotional influence by the users, rather than through adherence to the intellectual intent of the originators.

Just as the emphasis of the intellectual content can become secondary to the emotional content, a communication that is initially of an emotional nature can become more intellectually significant with the passage of time. For example, the religious symbol of the cross was originally used to communicate the emotional content of the crucifixion of Christ. In some situations, it was even used to ward off evil and protect the owner. Since then, the religious cross has become predominantly an intellectual symbol of Christianity. In this instance, emotional content has become secondary to intellectual content in the communication.

The combined presence of emotional and intellectual content in a visual or visual-verbal expression always increases the communication potential and possible response to an idea. And, if we are dealing with a large, diverse audience that does not share the same emotional and intellectual data, or if there is an eventual shift in emphasis from intellectual to emotional content or vice versa, this combination is very effective.

## How They Are Combined

Just as the reasons for combining emotional and intellectual content are important, so are the ways in which they are combined. When we are going to combine emotional and intellectual content to ensure optimum communication, the important questions to consider are these: What kind and how much of each is used in the combination? How can one form of content suggest the other? How specific can the communication be made? How can the alteration of one form modify or completely change the other? To obtain this optimum communication, it is necessary first to isolate and define the intellectual statement, and then to execute that statement with the appropriate emotional feeling so that the desired emotional and intellectual response will occur.

The quality and quantity of each form of content in an expression have a marked effect on the final communication. Any change in the quality or degree of the combination could modify the communication and the final response. For example, if one form of content diametrically opposes the other, this apparent contradiction can only transmit a message of confusion. Pink power tools, a stop sign that reads "Please Wait," or a Marine drill instructor who makes polite requests of

recruits rather than issuing commands are examples of combined emotional and intellectual content that are confusing in their communication. In each of these, the quality of either the emotional or the intellectual content is incorrect, so ultimately it diminishes the meaning of the other. In the case of the Marine drill instructor, the recruits may intellectually comprehend the instructor's unquestionable authority in relation to their training and conditioning. However, the instructor's unexpectedly polite behavior emotionally restricts the goal of teaching the recruits to respond accurately and immediately in situations of emergency.

In a more subtle way, the degree of each form of content combined in the communication affects the final response. This can be illustrated in the case of a typesetter who is given a job to be done. A single word of explanation—"Rush"—is written on the page. Intellectually, the typesetter would know that the job was intended to be completed quickly. The emotional response, however, could vary accordingly to the degree of emotional content apparent in the visual-verbal explanation. If the word "Rush" were very neatly printed in ornate letter forms, the typesetter may feel the job can wait while more pressing problems are taken care of first. On the other hand, if "Rush" were written in an almost illegible scrawl that emotionally communicated a sense of urgency, the typesetter would be more apt to give the task top priority and complete it immediately. From this illustration, it is easy to see how the degree of either form of content can greatly affect the final communication.

30

Magazine advertisement designed by Louis Danziger for Mamiya/Sekor, Courtesy Vivitar Corporation

30. This advertisement for a 35 MM camera is primarily intellectual in content. Since a camera is a highly technical device and technical products are a result of intellectual efforts, this is appropriate. Primarily, the intellectual communication is a photographic composite. Other secondary intellectual communications can also be seen: a contact sheet, a cross section of urban environments, images about a 35 MM camera that can be read in a left to right sequence. Additionally, since shooting random photos like those seen on the contact sheet is particularly entertaining for photographers, emotional content has also been incorporated into this communication.

In a similar way, the presence of either emotional or intellectual content in the expression can be used to suggest the other for a stronger form of communication. If a small boy gives his mother a gift of hand-picked wildflowers, the mother easily understands that the child is expressing his love for her. This communication is strong and succinct; the emotional and intellectual content work together to reinforce and strengthen one another. However, even if the gift of flowers were replaced by a cherished frog or a bouquet of weeds, the communication of "love" is still apparent regardless of the seeming inconsistency. Emotionally, the giving of the gift by the child to show love cannot be questioned, though intellectually the gift itself may be questionable. In this second instance, the emotional content so strongly suggests the intellectual intent that ultimately the communication potential is greater as a result of the combination.

All these ways of combining, adjusting, and controlling emotional and intellectual content are applicable to all areas of visual communication. An example of a work of studio art that utilizes combined emotional and intellectual content is *The State Hospital* by Edward Kienholz (Figure 33). Due to this content combination, it is possible to interpret this work as communicating a powerful and devastating statement. Initially, the title of the work provides a clue to the precise intellectual content. From this, it can be determined that *The State Hospital* intellectually deals with a social statement about institutionalized, emotionally ill people. Then, the addition of visual emotional content completes the communication in a specific way. The worn, chipped, flaking, once-white institutional metal beds with dirty, uncovered mattresses provide an emotional clue that more thoroughly defines the stated intellectual content. The emotional presentation of the type of human forms that are strapped to the beds further reinforces the intended communication. They are featureless, emaciated, and posed in attitudes that suggest utter submission, despair, and hopelessness. In fact, the only two clues that the figures are still alive are intellectual—the placement of the bedpan beneath the bed and the

31. In this sculpture, the artist has deliberately created a conflict in content. The intellectual communication is that of drinking. However, because the image is covered with fur, the senses are so assaulted that no one would want to drink from it.

32. The misspelling of the word "wait" significantly diminishes the intended intellectual communication of expertise and efficiency.

31

Meret Oppenheim, *Object,* 1936. Fur-covered cup, saucer, and spoon; cup, 4 3/8″ diameter; saucer, 9 3/8″ diameter; spoon, 8″ long; overall height 2 7/8″. Collection, The Museum of Modern Art, New York

32

Sign in a window of a shoe repair shop

"thought balloon" emanating from the figure on the bottom to envelop the figure on the top. Cumulatively, *The State Hospital* emotionally and intellectually communicates a statement that mental patients in contemporary society are imprisoned, cast away, forgotten—the living dead. This analysis illustrates how emotional and intellectual content work together to direct communication and obtain a specific response.

If some alterations were made in the emotional presentation of this work of art, the intellectual content could easily be modified or even completely changed.

For instance, if the institutional metal beds were freshly painted white, the mattresses were clean, and everything else was left unchanged, the emotional impact of the work would be significantly altered. But the intellectual content would be only slightly modified. However, if these clean mattresses were covered with black satin sheets, and the two original forms were replaced with voluptuous, beautiful humans strapped in an attitude of struggle, the emotional content would totally alter the intellectual content of the work. These examples show how drastically a communication can be affected by altering the degrees of emotional and intellectual content.

33

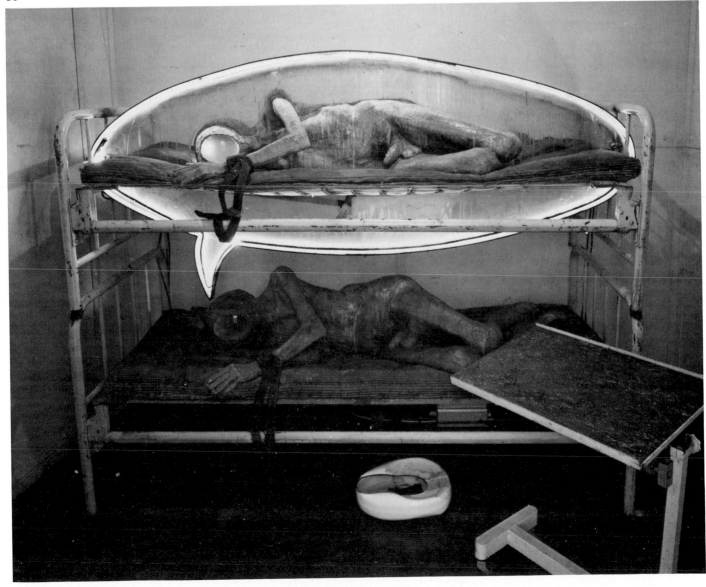

Edward Kienholz, *The State Hospital,* 1964–66. Collection, Moderna Museet, Stockholm

A slightly different use of emotional and intellectual content can be found in Tom Wesselmann's *Great American Nude #57* (Figure 34). Again, the title suggests the intellectual content—an American nude—but it does not spell it out as directly as Kienholz' *State Hospital*. Also, the emotional content is more subtle in this piece of Wesselmann's. Still, both forms work together to create a definite intellectual and emotional statement. Visual clues of hair, lips, nipples, and an indication of a bikini suntan all aid in the intellectual identification of a nude female figure. Reduction of the nude to these particular intellectual symbols, though, are what gives the work its emotional character. The combined emotional and intellectual presentation can be interpreted as communicating a particular segment of American society that is pursuing a "perfect" life, with particular attention to status, success, and commercialized sex. More simply, *Great American Nude #57* seems to be a statement about "packaged," production-line people—plastic, pristine, and cool. Again, as in Kienholz' *State Hospital,* this kind of complete communication occurs as a result of the artist's use of both emotional and intellectual content.

34

Tom Wesselmann, *Great American Nude #57,* 1964, synthetic polymer on composition board, 48″ x 65″.
Collection of Whitney Museum of American Art, Gift of Friends of the Whitney Museum of American Art

35

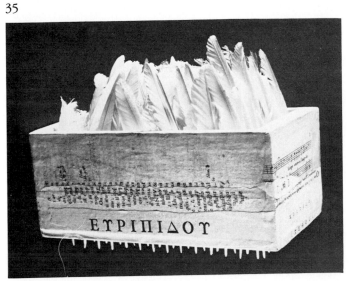

Lenore Tawney, *Album of White Music,*
Collection American Craft Museum. Photo Ferdinand Boesch

36

Wool Certification Mark,
Courtesy Wool Bureau

37. Rene Magritte, *The Lovers,* © ADAGP, Paris, 1981

35. The primary intellectual content is contained in the ancient writing and drawn musical notes. The secondary content is emotional and communicates poetic, lyrical feelings as well as provoking a tactile response.

36. This certification mark intellectually communicates a skein of yarn. The emotional content associated with the flowing, curvilinear lines and shapes of the image reinforces this.

37. *The Lovers*—an image of a couple kissing—intellectually communicates love. However, because there is no sensory exchange, the emotional content alters the intellectual and causes feelings of isolation.

The use of optimum combination is even more important in the applied arts, where direct, concise communication is almost always necessary. An excellent example of intellectual and emotional content can be found in a Container Corporation of America advertisement by the graphic designer Louis Danziger (Figure 39). Intellectually this advertisement presents a direct verbal quote about the idea of language. Then, the quote in combination with the speaking mouth and the repetitive random letter forms—the visual-verbal components of language—creates a secondary level of emotional content. In this case, the emotional content is that of power—power gleaned through one of humankind's greatest achievements, language. As a result, the intellectual and emotional content combine to elicit a strong, calculated response of intellectual comprehension and emotional feeling about the unlimited possibilities and ramifications of human language.

As this and all the previous examples illustrate, the combination of emotional and intellectual content can be a vital and effective tool in visual communications.

38. This building is intellectually identifiable as an airport. The intellectual function of the graceful form is also reinforced by its emotional content of a sense of soaring weightlessness.

38

Dulles Airport, Chantilly, VA, 1961–62, Architect Eero Saarinen. Ezra Stoller (c) ESTO

39

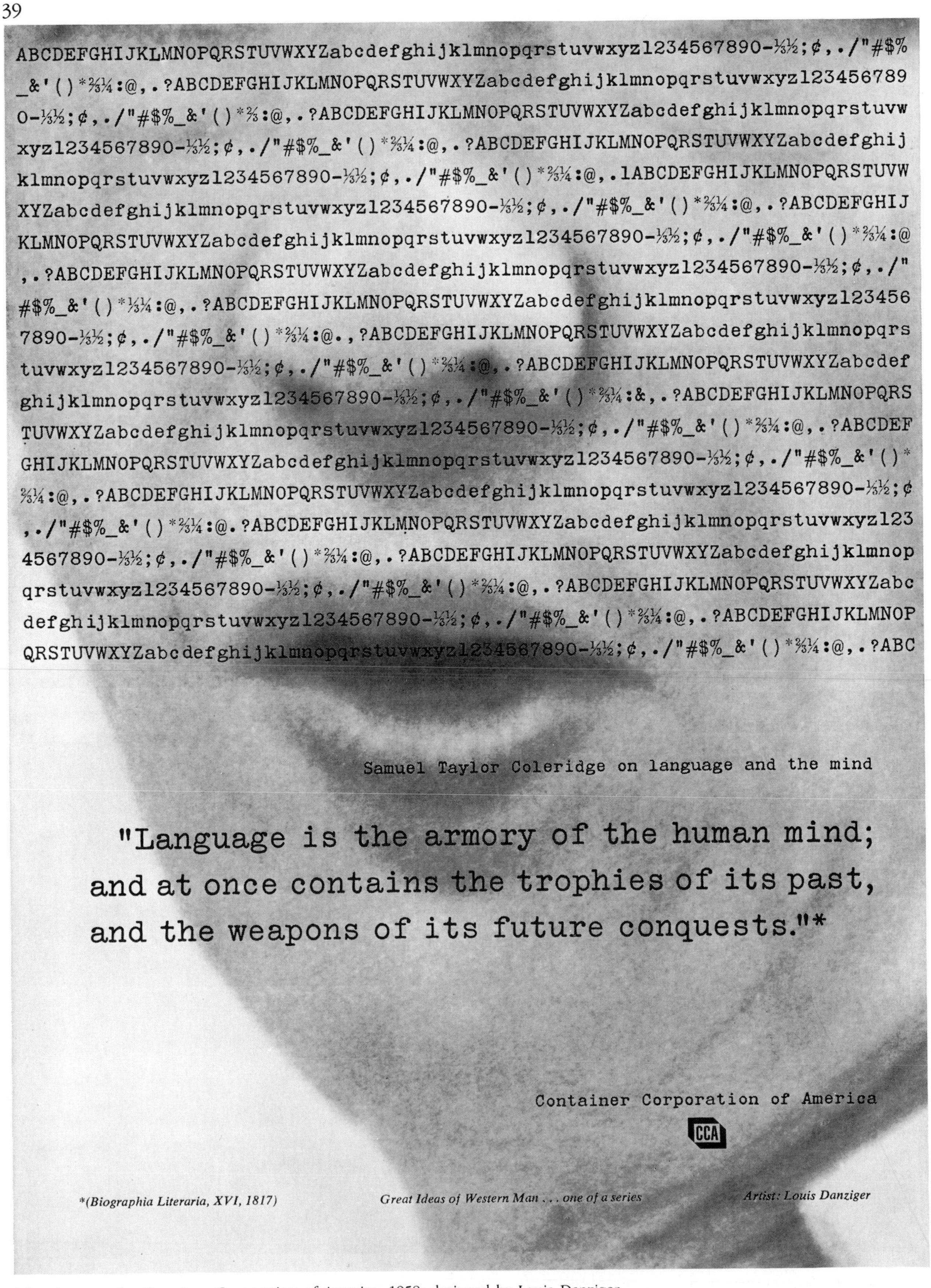

ABCDEFGHIJKLMNOPQRSTUVWXYZabcdefghijklmnopqrstuvwxyz1234567890-⅓½;¢,./"#$%_&'()*⅔¾:@,.?ABCDEFGHIJKLMNOPQRSTUVWXYZabcdefghijklmnopqrstuvwxyz123456789 0-⅓½;¢,./"#$%_&'()*⅔:@,.?ABCDEFGHIJKLMNOPQRSTUVWXYZabcdefghijklmnopqrstuvw xyz1234567890-⅓½;¢,./"#$%_&'()*⅔¾:@,.?ABCDEFGHIJKLMNOPQRSTUVWXYZabcdefghij klmnopqrstuvwxyz1234567890-⅓½;¢,./"#$%_&'()*⅔¾:@,.lABCDEFGHIJKLMNOPQRSTUVW XYZabcdefghijklmnopqrstuvwxyz1234567890-⅓½;¢,./"#$%_&'()*⅔¾:@,.?ABCDEFGHIJ KLMNOPQRSTUVWXYZabcdefghijklmnopqrstuvwxyz1234567890-⅓½;¢,./"#$%_&'()*⅔¾:@ ,.?ABCDEFGHIJKLMNOPQRSTUVWXYZabcdefghijklmnopqrstuvwxyz1234567890-⅓½;¢,./" #$%_&'()*⅓¾:@,.?ABCDEFGHIJKLMNOPQRSTUVWXYZabcdefghijklmnopqrstuvwxyz123456 7890-⅓½;¢,./"#$%_&'()*⅔¾:@,.?ABCDEFGHIJKLMNOPQRSTUVWXYZabcdefghijklmnopqrs tuvwxyz1234567890-⅓½;¢,./"#$%_&'()*⅔¾:@,.?ABCDEFGHIJKLMNOPQRSTUVWXYZabcdef ghijklmnopqrstuvwxyz1234567890-⅓½;¢,./"#$%_&'()*⅔¾:&,.?ABCDEFGHIJKLMNOPQRS TUVWXYZabcdefghijklmnopqrstuvwxyz1234567890-⅓½;¢,./"#$%_&'()*⅔¾:@,.?ABCDEF GHIJKLMNOPQRSTUVWXYZabcdefghijklmnopqrstuvwxyz1234567890-⅓½;¢,./"#$%_&'()* ⅔¾:@,.?ABCDEFGHIJKLMNOPQRSTUVWXYZabcdefghijklmnopqrstuvwxyz1234567890-⅓½;¢ ,./"#$%_&'()*⅔¾:@.?ABCDEFGHIJKLMNOPQRSTUVWXYZabcdefghijklmnopqrstuvwxyz123 4567890-⅓½;¢,./"#$%_&'()*⅔¾:@,.?ABCDEFGHIJKLMNOPQRSTUVWXYZabcdefghijklmnop qrstuvwxyz1234567890-⅓½;¢,./"#$%_&'()*⅔¾:@,.?ABCDEFGHIJKLMNOPQRSTUVWXYZabc defghijklmnopqrstuvwxyz1234567890-⅓½;¢,./"#$%_&'()*⅔¾:@,.?ABCDEFGHIJKLMNOP QRSTUVWXYZabcdefghijklmnopqrstuvwxyz1234567890-⅓½;¢,./"#$%_&'()*⅔¾:@,.?ABC

Samuel Taylor Coleridge on language and the mind

"Language is the armory of the human mind;
and at once contains the trophies of its past,
and the weapons of its future conquests."*

Container Corporation of America

*(Biographia Literaria, XVI, 1817)          Great Ideas of Western Man ... one of a series          Artist: Louis Danziger

Advertisement for Container Corporation of America, 1958; designed by Louis Danziger

# SECTION TWO

# 13

FUNDAMENTAL VISUAL COMMUNICATION METHODS

An infinite number of visual methods are used in art to transmit ideas. These techniques are not ideas in themselves, but rather are the visual means through which ideas are communicated. They can be controlled, modified, or altered individually or in an unlimited variety of combinations. We can classify these communication methods into seven fundamental categories: typography, representative images, image combination, narrative illustration, decorative images, image distortion/destruction, and sequential images.

1

Poster for the Nineteenth National Ceramic Exhibition,
Syracuse Museum of Fine Arts
designed by Chermayeff & Geismar Associates, New York

2

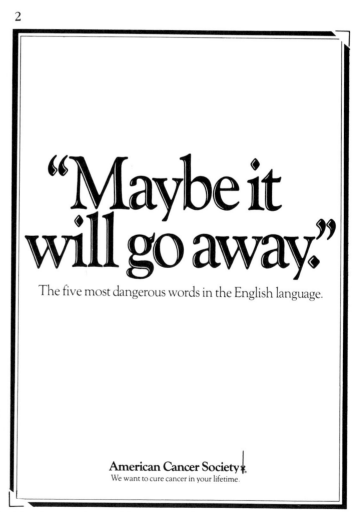

Advertisement designed by Benton & Bowles
for American Cancer Society, Inc.

## TYPOGRAPHY

The visual method that probably communicates most directly to an educated audience is typography—the use of printed words or copy. Frequently, artists use the visual character of letter forms as abstract or nonobjective shapes to dramatize a visual expression. For example, the visual impact of a poster design by Chermayeff and Geismar (Figure 1) relies completely on the abstract character of letter forms. To create this impact, the letter forms have been magnified in such a way that their abstract qualities draw attention to the intended intellectual communication. In comparison, Figure 2 demonstrates typography's potential of communicating verbal information regardless of its visual character.

Using particular kinds of words can be very effective in drawing attention to a typographic communication. The announcement for a Dallas Society of Visual Communication Talent Show (Figure 3) uses humorous copy to communicate to its intended audience.

Typography is commonly associated with the applied arts of advertising and graphic design, but it is also used effectively in studio art. In his series of prints entitled *Great Moments in Domestic Mishaps,* Lynwood Kreneck presents everyday, mundane occurrences as newspaper stories with datelines and body copy. Figure 4, which is a part of that series, reads, "CACTUS VALLEY ARIZONA. An Arizona woman who dropped an unusual egg, finds herself the focus of local and federal attention...." These series of prints are excellent examples of how copy can be used in studio art expressions.

3

4

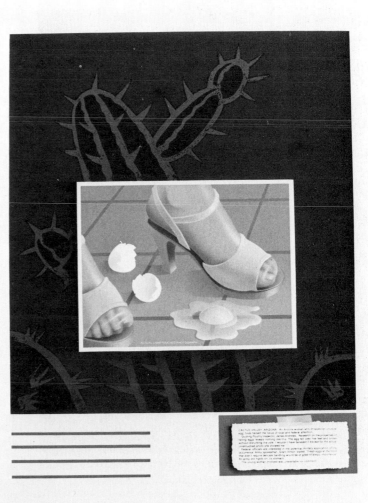

Sure,
you can draw,
but can you
make funny noises
with your hands?

There is an old saying about talent:
Those who can, do. Those who can't,
teach. And those who can't do either one,
try it at the DSVC Talent Show.
Try it yourself on June 4. Sing. Dance.
Do impressions with your thighs.

Call Sam Johnson at 620-7255 and
he'll reserve for you all the time you need
to strut your stuff.

P.S. Since six people have already listed
their talent as "Dueling Moons," a
moon-off will be held at Mack Boles'
studio next Saturday.

Announcement designed by Bob Holman/Sam Johnson, Courtesy of The Creative Dept., Inc.

Lynwood Kreneck, *Great Moments in Domestic Mishaps/The Broken Egg.* Collection, Arkansas Art Center

## REPRESENTATIVE IMAGES

To use this visual technique, a recognizable image is selected that represents a particular category. Frequently, representative imagery is presented along with a verbal message that identifies or clarifies the category. This combination of a visual and verbal message may be necessary to make the visual communication clear and specific.

The poster design in Figure 5 would be merely a visual presentation of a frog's skeleton without the typographic designation, "Cincinnati Museum of Natural History." Once this verbal communication is made, the visual image becomes representative of the broad category of natural history—even though it is only one of many relevant natural images.

Without the title, the communication of Duane Hanson's lifelike sculpture (Figure 6) of an unattractive, middle-aged couple would be nonspecific. However, accompanied by the title *The Tourists*, the representative image of the couple specifically becomes a satirical statement about a particular segment of contemporary American society.

Representative images are used in advertising to communicate vital information to mass audiences. The public service advertment for the American Cancer Society uses representative imagery and reinforcing copy to communicate important information. The image, in this case, represents self-examination for breast cancer, and the copy describes the importance of such a process (Figure 7).

5

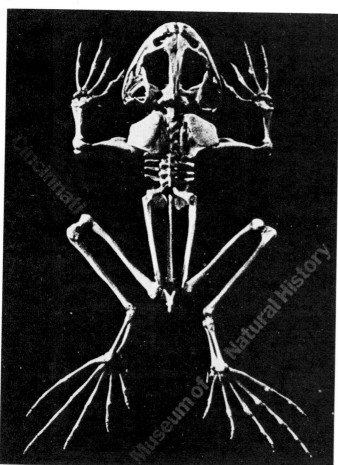

Poster by Joseph Bottoni and Bill Sontag for Cincinnati Museum of Natural History. Courtesy Cincinnati Chamber of Commerce

6

Duane Hanson, *Tourists,* 1970,
Courtesy OK Harris Works of Art, New York

In the form of a trademark, representative imagery is often used to communicate a particular company's product or service. The archery symbol in Figure 8, for instance, is used to represent both archery equipment and its functions, since it derives its form from an arrow fletch and a deer track.

Finally, representative images have been used throughout history to represent events of religious significance. Figure 9 represents the celebration of Xipe Totec, the Aztec god of fertility. The ceremony consisted of the sacrifice and flaying of a person of high birth. This was followed by a priest's donning of the skin to symbolize the rebirth of the god and, in turn, the rebirth of the soil and the attendant crops. In Figure 9, a priest is represented wearing the skin of the sacrificial victim.

8

Trademark for Ben Pearson Archery, designed by Frank Cheatham
Courtesy Ben Pearson Archery Company

7

This space contributed by the publisher as a public service.

Photograph by Hal Davis

# Take your life in your own hands.

Nine out of ten breast cancers are discovered by women themselves.
If you're not already examining your breasts because you don't know how, any doctor or qualified nurse will be glad to help you.
Breast self-examination is a gentle art of self-defense. It takes only a few minutes a month. It's simpler and faster than putting on your eye make-up. And certainly more important.
Think about it before you turn the page. Nothing you can do for yourself is as easy or has as much effect on your future health and happiness.
We want to cure cancer in your lifetime.
Give to the American Cancer Society.

## American Cancer Society

Advertisement by Benton & Bowles for American Cancer Society, Inc.

9

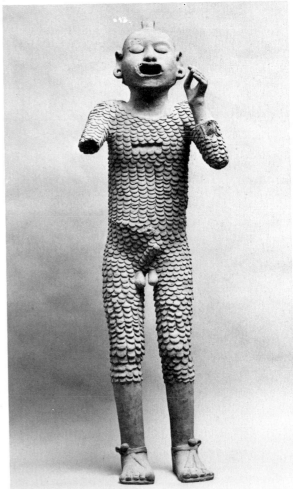

Figure of Xipe Totec. Americas, Aztec, Puebla.
The Metropolitan Museum of Art,
Michael C. Rockefeller Memorial Collection,
Gift of Nelson A. Rockefeller, 1978

## IMAGE COMBINATION

Another visual communication method is image combination—the combining of two or more images by juxtaposition. Usually, the combination of the images is done in a way that changes or alters their original individual meanings without completely destroying them. In most cases, the combined images affect one another to the extent that the visual, as well as the communicative, results are more dramatic, intriguing, and unusual than they were before the images were combined.

There are two basic types of image combination: each one is created by a slightly different form of juxtaposition. One form places disparate objects side by side in the same frame of reference in such a way that although they retain their own unaltered identity, their relationship is new and unexpected. René Magritte has used this form of image combination in a painting, *Personal Values* (Figure 10), to make a visual expression that is dramatic and conceptually intriguing. Another example of this form of image combination can be seen in a cover for a German cultural magazine featuring an article on Mao's new revolution (Figure 11). This illustration creates a portrait of the Chinese leader by juxtaposing thousands of tiny Chinese people in various attitudes at certain distances from one another. The overall configuration of the face is formed, while each figure retains its individual identity.

10

Rene Magritte, *Personal Values.* (c) ADAGP, Paris 1981

Illustration by Hans-Georg Rauch for *En Masse*. Permission of Macmillan Publishing Co., Inc., (c) Rowoholt Verlag GmbH, 1974

The other type of image combination uses a different form of juxtaposition. With this method, disparate objects are combined in such a way that they appear physically attached. Each object retains enough of its visual character to remain recognizable, but in combination each is altered enough to create a new and often unusual image. *The Collective Invention* by Magritte (Figure 12) joins a fish with a human body in such a smooth transition that the combination seems disturbingly natural. In Figures 13 and 14, unusual effects are created by combining images through less smooth but equally effective transitions. In Figure 13, a pen point is combined with a serpentine body to create a fanciful snake that visually represents and reinforces the typographic communication—"The Poison Pen." And in Figure 14, a red, white, and blue drawing of an American flag is superimposed over a paintbrush to represent and announce an exhibition of American painting at the Los Angeles County Museum of Art.

12

Rene Magritte, *The Collective Invention.* (c) ADAGP, Paris 1981

13

Poster designed by Milton Glaser,
Courtesy Visual Arts Gallery, New York

14

Poster for Los Angeles County Museum of Art, 1966.
Designer Louis Danziger

## NARRATIVE ILLUSTRATION

Narrative illustration utilizes recognizable, pictorial imagery to tell a story, describe a circumstance, or visualize an object.

An example of all three forms of narrative illustration can be seen in the visual images prehistoric people used to illustrate aspects of their world that were important to survival—the hunt, the animals they hunted, and so on. Since these early artists first used narrative illustration to record important events and objects, its nature and function has not changed essentially except in media selection and presentation. Today, effective narrative illustrations can be executed in any possible media or process. They can consist of photographs, stylized drawings or paintings, collages, highly decorative or whimsical works, sculpture, and so on.

Many extraordinary works of art use narrative illustrations even though they incorporate other qualities as well. For example, Edward Hopper's painting *The Night Hawks* (Figure 15) exhibits narrative illustration because it depicts a city scene with social symbolism—an all night diner and the people who frequent it. However, this painting does more than just describe one event; it comments on a phenomenon of city life and perhaps society in general. The painting's lack of specific descriptive detail, as well as a strong feeling of isolation and loneliness, give it a universal quality that results in a dynamic, powerful work of art.

15

Edward Hopper, *Nighthawks*, 1942, Courtesy The Art Institute of Chicago

In comparison, professional illustrators in the applied arts often create narrative illustration with the intent of telling a specific story, describing a circumstance, or visualizing an object. These artists are concerned with communicating a particular message to a certain audience in a visually exciting way. An excellent example of this can be seen in a book cover illustration by Bart Forbes for *Paths of Glory* (Figure 16). This illustration is a sensitive, skilled distillation and presentation of a story set in France during World War I. Another example of the effective and successful use of narrative illustration can be seen in Figure 17. By illustrating the contents of this package with a photograph, the artist solved a costly display and sales problem for the manufacturer. When assembled, the crossbow was too large to package and ship economically, so it had to be packaged disassembled. Realistically, unless it could be seen assembled, no one would buy it. The use of narrative illustration in the form of a photograph effectively solved this problem.

16

17

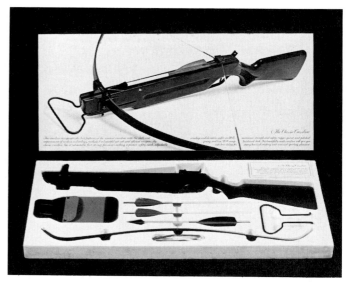

Package for Classic Cross Bow designed by Frank Cheatham

Illustration by Bart Forbes

## DECORATIVE IMAGES

Decorative visual expressions often use basic visual design elements to communicate pleasurable emotional or emotional and intellectual messages. In some cases, decoration or embellishment is used in a work of art to provide visual stimulation only. This form of decoration is not intended to communicate a specific idea. But many artists have used decorative methods to express and communicate profound and meaningful ideas. The distinction between decorative as a goal in and of itself, and decorative as a means toward a goal, is subtle but significant. For example, the various decorative items in Tutankhamen's tomb might be dismissed by some as ornamental objects with only historical or monetary value. Actually, these decorative visual expressions were created to communicate deeply felt religious concerns.

And to this day they still transmit a pleasurable emotional message to a large audience that considers them remarkable works of art.

The British painter Alan Davie consistently expresses his concepts through decorative images. A painter, musician, poet, glider pilot, mystic, and romantic, Davie is a modern Merlin who imparts his feelings about the mysteries of life in delightful, powerful, and often magical visual expressions. These qualities can be seen in his painting *Trio for Flute, Dog, and Ram* (Figure 18).

18

Alan Davie, *Trio for Ram, Flute and Dog,* 1961, Collection Phoenix Art Museum, Gift of Mr. James P. Upham

In a similar way, decorative methods can be used in the applied arts. A rocking chair designed by Gebruder Thonet (Figure 19) is a marvelous example of decorative design with emotional content. The chair's visual ornamentation serves a purpose—structural support. Also, the flowing curves are emotionally consistent with the feeling experienced when using a rocking chair.

Decorative imagery with content is exemplified in the Cuna Indian mola in Figure 20. The mola is actually a blouse that is worn by the natives of the San Blas Islands located near the mainland of Panama. To these people, the mola not only displays skillful, decorative needlework, but represents the extent of individual wealth as well. A young Cuna woman includes as many molas as possible in her dowry.

20

Mola, Peru. Private Collection

19

Gebrüder Thonet, Rocking chair, 1960. Bent beechwood: cane, 37 1/2″ height. Collection, The Museum of Modern Art, New York, Gift of Café Nicholson

## IMAGE DISTORTION/DESTRUCTION

The term *image distortion/destruction* is self-explanatory—it refers to the visual distortion or destruction of an image. In certain situations, visual images are deliberately distorted or partially destroyed to aid in the communication of a particular concept. Deliberate distortion and partial destruction can be used in drawings, paintings, illustrations, photographs, sculptures, typography, and so on. In addition, image distortion/destruction can communicate a broad range of emotional, intellectual, and combined intellectual and emotional content.

The use of image distortion/destruction in photography can be seen in the advertisement for *Fortune* magazine (Figure 21). Dramatic visual impact is imparted through the use of this technique. This, in turn, reinforces the emotional and intellectual content of the message contained in the headline and body copy.

21

Advertisement for *Fortune* magazine

22

Francis Bacon, *Head Surrounded by Sides of Beef,* 1954. Collection Art Institute Chicago

Some studio artists so consistently use intentional image distortion/destruction as a method of communicating their concepts that the method is associated with their style. Two such artists, Francis Bacon and Fernando Botero, use this method to achieve entirely different results. Francis Bacon uses intentional image distortion/destruction to express powerful, demonic, or monstrous images that are disturbing or horrifying. *Head Surrounded by Sides of Beef* (Figure 22) is a fine example of Bacon's tormented but exciting expressions. In comparison, Fernando Botero uses image distortion/destruction to create images that seem to be caricatures of portraits by Rubens and Velasquez, as in *Rubens' Woman* (Figure 23). Unlike Bacon's paintings, which

leave no doubt that horror is part of the intended communication, the viewer is not always sure whether Botero's exaggerated figures are intended to create a comic or a grotesque effect.

Image distortion/destruction is effectively used in the illustration for a book dealing with schizophrenia (Figure 24). By distorting the figure to suggest a simultaneous coming and going, a schizophrenic—the root word "schizo" means split or division—condition is symbolized.

23

Fernando Botero, *Ruben's Woman*, 1963.
The Solomon R. Guggenheim Museum
Collection, N.Y.

24

Cathy Hull/Jules Perlmutter,
from *Abnormal Psychology* published by John Wiley & Sons, Inc.

## SEQUENTIAL IMAGES

Another visual communication method is the use of images in a sequence to create the effect of movement, change, relativity, time, space, distance, or growth. This technique can be called *sequential images.* (Sequential imagery that specifically relates to time, change, and motion is discussed in detail in Chapter 8.) Sequential imagery has the potential to communicate varied amounts and types of information relative to the effects mentioned above.

Images in sequence through the combination of two- and three-dimensional media is exemplified in Figure 25. In this intriguing work by James Broderick, there is a series of five photographs framed on the top and bottom by a series of smaller sequential images. The middle series depicts—from left to right—a man smoking a cigarette, exhaling a smoke ring, catching the ring in a tube, and then sealing both ends of the tube with wax. The conclusion of this action is found in the form of the actual wax-sealed tube in which, presumably, the smoke ring might still exist. In this work, the artist has not only effectively expressed time, change, and motion, but he has left the viewer with a provocative question.

25

James Broderick, *Capture and Containment of a Smoke Ring,* 1977. Courtesy of the artist

## CONCLUSION

As we have frequently emphasized, in application all the design components—tangible and intangible—are so interrelated that they are actually inseparable. However, in our discussions we have continually isolated these components to provide a better understanding of their properties and uses. Now that this has been done for each—gestalt, idea, composition, communication, and so on—it is possible to synthesize them so we can view and apply them as a whole.

We have seen that the tangible components of design are the visual vocabulary of art. Therefore, learning to use this vocabulary effectively is a necessary part of our growth as artists. For instance, very often the product of a beginning design exercise is considered successful if it demonstrates an effective visual manipulation of a specified design element. Eventually, however, this focus on any particular tangible design element becomes subordinated to a larger concern as we begin to feel the need to create something more than a visual exercise. At this time, we begin combining the tangible components of design with the intangible ones—idea, communication, and content—to obtain a more complete form of creative expression.

By putting it all together, we not only have a more complete understanding of how to design, but we have a firmer foundation on which to base our work. We can begin to recognize our own special abilities, take pride in our contributions, and enjoy our imaginative flights of fancy. Once we can formulate strong ideas and effectively communicate them through the implementation of tangible processes, as artists we become capable of creating anything that we wish to express.

# INDEX